The Philosophical Irony
of Laurence Sterne

The Philosophical Irony

of Laurence Sterne

HELENE MOGLEN

A UNIVERSITY OF FLORIDA BOOK

THE UNIVERSITY PRESSES OF FLORIDA
Gainesville · 1975

Part Four first appeared in *The Winged Skull: Bicentenary Papers on Laurence Sterne*, edited by A. H. Cash and John M. Stedmond (The Kent State University Press, 1971), and is republished by permission.

Library of Congress Cataloging in Publication Data

Moglen, Helene, 1936–
  The philosophical irony of Laurence Sterne.

  "A University of Florida book."
  "Part four first appeared in The winged skull: bicentenary papers on Laurence Sterne, edited by A. H. Cash and John M. Stedmond."
  Bibliography: p.
  Includes index.
  1. Sterne, Laurence, 1713–1768. The life and opinions of Tristram Shandy, gentleman. 2. Sterne, Laurence, 1713–1768—Humor, satire, etc. 3. Irony in literature. I. Title.
PR3714.T73M6   823'.6   75–4574
ISBN 0–8130–0363–6

A University of Florida Book

COPYRIGHT © 1975 BY THE BOARD OF REGENTS OF THE STATE OF FLORIDA

PRINTED BY THE ROSE PRINTING COMPANY, INCORPORATED
TALLAHASSEE, FLORIDA

Acknowledgments

To Martin Price, in whose class I first studied *The Life and Opinions of Tristram Shandy* and under whose direction I wrote the dissertation which ultimately became this book, I owe the largest debt of gratitude. To Morris Golden, who read the completed manuscript and offered invaluable criticism and support, I am also greatly indebted.

Arthur Cash has occupied a special place in the history of this effort. It was he who first read, as a separate essay, the final chapter of the book and, with John Stedmond, invited me to present it at the Laurence Sterne Bicentenary Conference which met at the University of York, September 2–5, 1968. The papers, the discussions, the extraordinarily positive sense I had of my fellow Sterneans—all of this was stimulating and exciting and renewed my enthusiasm for my work.

To my oldest son, Eben, who acted on several occasions as editor, I owe my appreciation for his patience and care. To my younger sons, Damon and Seth, who graciously accepted Tristram as still another sibling with whom they had to share their mother's attention, I offer apologies and love. And to Sig, my husband, whose faith in the project might have faltered, but never his faith in my ability to accomplish it nor his willingness to help in whatever ways made that accomplishment possible, I offer the fruit of our mutual labor.

To My Parents
Who Made Everything Possible

Contents

The Ironic Philosopher

Laurence Sterne was a prophet. Like most prophets he has appeared before the less visionary in the accoutrements of madness. To some his madness has seemed to share in the fabled divinity of the poet. To others it has partaken of Satanic confusion and chaos. Surely many would agree that his vision has been fulfilled in our own time, but even they must acknowledge that the validity of the vision has still to be confirmed. *Tristram Shandy* can be seen as the *Finnegans Wake* of the eighteenth century, and it remains as paradoxical to its sympathizers and as distasteful to the orthodox as it was at the time of its publication in 1759.

The paradox begins, not unsuitably, in that very area to which the critic frequently turns first: the life, the personality, the attitude of the author. Laurence Sterne is not the least cryptic of his own creations, and to differentiate between the creation and the man is a difficult task. The facts of his life are deceptively simple.[1] Born in 1713, the son of an Irish army officer, Sterne was educated haphazardly and ingloriously, was married unhappily but not tragically, and was urged into the church by the considerations of a practical head rather than by the dictates of a deeply committed heart. His life did not move in a crescendo of crises. Two of its most significant events presented themselves when he was still a student at Cambridge: his introduction to Locke's *An Essay Concerning Human Understanding* and his first attack of tuberculosis, the disease which was to cast its shadow over all of his years. For the rest, but for two brief tours on the continent and occasional visits to London, he lived for twenty years as a country parson, in a village eight miles north of York, amid domestic and ecclesiastical squabbles and petty economic problems.

1. Wilbur L. Cross, *The Life and Times of Laurence Sterne*, remains the best, most thorough biography of Sterne.

Biographical notes have always marked him a dabbler with regard to his relationships and his interests. With his wife he maintained, at best, an armed peace. Toward his daughter, Lydia, he played the role of a fond but little-respected advisor. His friendships with members of artistic and intellectual circles never seemed to develop beyond the superficial. He "tried" painting and music much as he did gardening: investing sufficient time and energy to gain some degree of proficiency, but never committing himself enough to become a master. When writing his sermons he found it most convenient to gather material from the published efforts of other clergymen.[2] The original contributions that he made had little to do with matters of doctrine but were concerned with the embellishment of character. He read as a dilettante: not widely and, it would seem, not deeply. In his favorite authors—Rabelais, Cervantes, Burton, Montaigne, Erasmus, Bacon, and Swift—he recognized the great diversity of literary styles capable of expressing the fecundity and richness of the human mind. But from his autobiographical and semi-autobiographical writings we have no sense of how his own literary theories developed, no knowledge of his growth as an author or, for that matter, as a man; no feeling for the relation of *Tristram Shandy* to his personal conflicts or abilities. His letters are never intimate. They reveal nothing of his interior life. Less revealing still is the series of self-portraits offered in *Tristram Shandy* and *A Sentimental Journey*. In these there is little hope of separating the person from the persona, the poseur from the posture. His *Journal to Eliza*, frequently treated as the frantic outpouring of a morbidly love-sick heart, seems rather to contain the most exaggerated and self-conscious set of attitudes to be found anywhere in his work.

One must finally conclude that Sterne never created a more successful paradox than that protean image of himself which he constantly transmuted in the distorting mirror of his art. Like the fascinating court jester, the wise fool, Sterne lives curiously without a private life, the quality of his interior self only implied by his public statements. He is acceptable as a social critic because he confronts society as an outcast, eccentric and solitary, without place or investment.

It is not accidental, then, that Sterne presents his two personae, Tristram and Yorick, as jester figures. They are the proper spokes-

---

2. Lansing Hammond, *Laurence Sterne's Sermons of Mr. Yorick*, offers a fine, detailed study of Sterne's sources.

men for his belief that "everything in the world is big with jest,——
and has wit in it, and instruction too, if we can but find it out."[3] It
is as the jester that Tristram speaks when he explains, "I sat down
to write my life for the amusement of the world, and my opinions
for its instruction" (III.xxviii.265). To amuse and to instruct: these
are the jester's functions. But Sterne, Tristram, and the jester all
knew that it would be inadequate to amuse alone, intolerable to
instruct directly. They could only instruct by amusing and to do this
they had to implicate their audiences in contradiction, force them
to participate with riddles, insults, cajolery, ambiguity, and love.
They had to set problems of interpretation which would not easily
be solved, problems for which there might be no single answer, as
Sterne suggests in a letter to an American admirer: "Your walking
stick is in no sense more Shandaick, than in that of its having more
handles than one: the parallel breaks only in this, that in using the
stick, everyone will take the handle which suits his convenience. In
Tristram Shandy, the handle is taken which suits their passions,
their ignorance, or their sensibility."[4]

For Sterne all knowledge—rational, emotional, and imaginative—
is subjective. Each man makes his world conform to his own pleasure and predisposition. The result is a simplification and distortion
of reality. All experience is essentially ironic in nature. That which
is most explicitly or obviously presented as truth is usually an inversion of another truth, a more basic truth, which is hidden but
implied. But, because there is never an absolute truth (only a number of possible points of view which must be balanced against one
another) statements, people, appearances are not simply the opposites of what they seem. They are themselves *and* their opposites.
The problem which the reader faces in approaching *Tristram Shandy*
is identical to the problem he faces day by day, mystery inside
ambiguity, in the maze of his own life. Sterne calls upon him to
relate to the novel as he must relate to any part of his own experience. For the novel, like the jester's riddle, is as complex, ambiguous,
paradoxical—as humorous and absurd—as life itself. Upon the mind
purged by confusion and cleansed by laughter Sterne impresses a
new vision of reality which contains within itself a simplifying truth
about the nature of man, who aspires despite his limitations, who

3. Laurence Sterne, *The Life and Opinions of Tristram Shandy, Gentleman*,
ed. James A. Work (New York, 1940), Volume V, chapter xxxii, p. 393. All
subsequent references will be to this edition and will be given in the text.
4. Laurence Sterne, "To Dr. John Eustace, Feb. 9, 1768," *Letters*, p. 411.

persists despite his defeats, who, though locked in isolation, is still capable of loving.

The overriding irony of the work derives from the relation of the apparent confusion of form and theme to the actual structural and conceptual order. The close parallel between Sterne's theory of art and his philosophical view of reality must again be mentioned. The experienced world is made up of random impressions which are given meaning by the perceiving eye. Similarly, a man's life, Sterne tells us through his characterizations, appears to the observer to be little more than eccentricity and chaos. But the appearance cloaks a principle of organization bestowed by the coherence of the individual's personality. The most bizarre fantasies, the most illogical associations, reveal their internal logic to anyone who can project himself into the wonderland of another's mind. Instead of abnormality there is only a variety of different perspectives.

All of life, Sterne seems to say, is an irony; each man who lives it is an ironist—his functioning largely unconscious—for he composes the mysteries of those appearances which are extensions of himself. But each man is therefore his own enemy, victim of the ironist within, alienated as he attempts to unravel the secret of his own identity as well as the identities of others. To write as Sterne does is to consciously imitate life while standing apart from it. It is to become the ironist as jester, not wholly part of society, not completely human. Sterne creates Tristram, who stands between the ironist and the victim, the writer and the reader, the creator and the interpreter. In him, on a human and fallible level, both partial selves come together, and living and writing are joined in the same mysterious function.

Tristram Shandy is, then, an astonishing reflection of reality, of its discontinuity as well as its coherence. It is an elaborately formed complex of interrelated ironic patterns which belong to the fundamental ironic concept. The purpose of this study of Sterne's philosophical irony is to consider the sources of Sterne's vision and its expression through the novel's forms, characters, and themes. But the final word will belong to the creator rather than to the interpreter. It is for him to point to the ultimate truth and the ultimate irony: "But *Tristram Shandy*, my friend, was made and formed to baffle all criticism—and I will venture to rest the book on this ground,—that it is either above the power or beneath the attention of any critic or hyper-critic whatsoever."[5]

5. Ibid.

One

John Locke, the Hero
of Tristram Shandy

I shall begin, in the Shandean way, with a paradox: "A critical study of *Tristram Shandy* must have as its first step a careful analysis of the epistemology of John Locke." Like most of the Shandean paradoxes, this contains a large measure of truth, for Sterne's themes, his technique, perhaps even his motivation for writing the novel, came from his reading of *An Essay Concerning Human Understanding*.[1] Tristram himself suggests to the reader the rather unusual bias of his own work when he describes Locke's *Essay*: "I will tell you in three words what the book is.——It is a history.——A history! of who? what? where? when? Don't hurry yourself.——It is a history-book, Sir, (which may possibly recommend it to the world) of what passes in a man's own mind; and if you will say so much of the book, and no more, believe me, you will cut no contemptible figure in a metaphysic circle" (II.ii.85). But if this is an appropriate introduction to Tristram's book, as it is an apt description of Locke's work, it is also misleading in its simplicity and invites the kind of appraisal that James A. Work offers in the introduction to his edition of *Tristram Shandy*: "But though a great reader, Sterne was not a great thinker. His mind was alert and facile, and he displayed at times an intuitive logic, but he lacked the power of deep and sustained thought. His intellect was at the

1. I am indebted to John Traugott's excellent study, *Tristram Shandy's World*, for providing the initial impetus for my approach and for offering much help along the way. In my discussion, I have attempted to emphasize areas of influence which Traugott seems to treat inadequately, and I have tried to suggest, as Traugott does not, ways in which Sterne used Locke's philosophy as an aesthetic tool. Our most extreme differences arise from the fact that Traugott denies that *Tristram Shandy* is a novel, preferring to define it as an exercise in philosophical rhetoric (this view has recently been amplified by Melvyn New, *Laurence Sterne as Satirist*) while I examine the ways in which Sterne's interpretation of Locke forced him to create a novel form that could be considered in its relation to earlier traditions of fiction.

9

mercy of his sensibility, and he created no ideas of significance" (xxiii). Work has fallen into the ready trap of confusing Sterne the creator with Tristram the creation. His judgment can be applied validly to Tristram, but it is imperceptive as a description of the novelist himself.

A close reading of *Tristram Shandy* as a history of the human mind in its particular and universal manifestations reveals Sterne to be more than a naïve disciple of Locke, and the abstract hypotheses of the novel demand that Sterne be taken seriously as a perceptive and creative critic of philosophy. Tristram speaks, in a sense, for both novelist and philosopher when he says: "But mark, Madam, we live amongst riddles and mysteries——the most obvious things, which come in our way, have dark sides, which the quickest sight cannot penetrate into; and even the clearest and most exalted understandings amongst us find ourselves puzzled and at a loss in almost every cranny of nature's works; so that this, like a thousand other things, falls out for us in a way, which tho' we cannot reason upon it,—— yet we find the good of it, may it please your reverences and your worships——and that's enough for us" (IV.xvii.293). Tristram here is echoing Locke's awareness of the "riddles and mysteries," of the "dark sides" of things, while sharing Locke's sense of the ultimate limitations of the human understanding. The proofs are all about them—not least in the failure of communication. The self-confidence of the rational philosopher is at every point undermined by the sceptical, commonsense observations of the realistic observer. The *Essay*, as we shall see, is full of such qualifications, contradictions, and uneasy compromises between the old rationalism and the new empiricism. But Locke, despite all, continues to place his hope in reason, in the power of the mind to master the abstract, to order experience, to give scientific validity to the concept of God if to nothing else.

Sterne's optimism is more limited, his scepticism more thorough. He seeks and frequently finds "the good of it," but his assurance "that's enough for us" seems in the context of the novel more than a little rueful and perhaps even tragic. Comprehending the nature of Locke's intellectual problem, admiring the aspirations and achievements of the *Essay*, and translating many aspects of the epistemology into fictional terms, Sterne remained principally interested in Locke's own paradoxical position, the unsteady bridge he constructed between two impossible alternatives: the analytic functioning of reason and man's domination by his senses. "The good of it," for Sterne, could not be derived from the functioning of the rational faculty. It was not the result of education and self-discipline. It lay instead in man's capacity for commonsense response and in his instinctual reaching out in mute sympathy toward his fellows. It did not allow for the progressive development of rational potentialities in which Locke wanted to believe. It drew value from the rare and fleeting moment of emotionally determined response.

✤

An examination of the sources of Locke's philosophy reveals that his basic dilemma grew out of an intellectual impasse of the time. Ernest Tuveson calls it the "paradox of a subjective psychology in an age of objective science."[2] Locke was presented on one side with the comprehensive natural laws of Newton—an ordered universe which lay open to the fallible but probing, rational mind. On the other side, he was aware of the incongruities, the contradictions, the seemingly gratuitous nature of men's ideas, so obviously grounded in the relativity of the empirical world. To discover a psychology of valid laws while maintaining man in the natural environment of his senses—this was his task. It was necessary to mediate between the mechanism of Hobbes, which imprisoned man in the determinism of the material world, and the pure rationalism of Descartes, which (with its insistence upon innate ideas) sharply divided intellection from perception and imagination.[3] He had to indicate the ways in which the functioning of the mind, while often fallible in its subjectivity, was nevertheless intelligible.

Locke begins by maintaining that all ideas originate in sensation or reflection and are of two distinct types, simple and complex. Denying with the other leading theorists of the period the reality of the universal, Locke emphasizes in his theory of the "tabula rasa" the way in which the mind—essentially passive and unable to avoid perception—acts as a mirror in its reception of the particular image: "The senses at first let in particular ideas, and furnish the yet empty cabinet, and the mind by degrees growing familiar with some of them, they are lodged in the memory, and names got to them. Afterwards, the mind proceeding further, abstracts them, and by degrees

2. *The Imagination as a Means of Grace*, p. 26.
3. Ernest L. Tuveson, "Locke and the Dissolution of the Ego," pp. 159–60.

learns the use of general names."[4] The mind forms its complex ideas voluntarily. The process is a result of combining, comparing, and abstracting simple ideas in order to construct ideas of modes, relation, and substance (I.ii.xii.1–3;213–15).

Locke's tendency to maintain simultaneously a view of learning that is orderly and objective, yet psychological and subjective, involved him in a curious dilemma. He is unwilling to follow the implications of his epistemology, which would involve an acceptance of the creative functioning of the mind in accordance with its own laws—the basis of Kant's theory of knowledge—and he persists instead in defining learning as discovery or apprehension. The fundamental problem is therefore one of subjectivity, and it is concerned with the relation of the idea to the reality, of the nominal to the real essence. Since he begins with the concept of a mind initially empty, he cannot suggest a way of testing either the correlation between the simple idea and the external reality or the correctness of the construction of the complex idea.

Because man is dependent for his knowledge upon his senses and the information which he can generalize from his observations and reflections, it follows that he can never be sure of the correspondence of his concepts to the real world. Still, speaking of primary qualities (those qualities which are inseparable from the body, such as solidity, extension, figure, motion or rest, and number [I.ii.viii.9; 169]) Locke does at times imply that things do actually have those qualities which they *appear* to possess: that ideas of primary qualities are resemblances of patterns that exist in the bodies themselves, while the perception of secondary qualities (color, sound, smell, etc.) is dependent upon our senses (I.ii.viii.15;173). As Berkeley points out, Locke has no more reason for maintaining the objective reference of the first category of concepts than he has for the second.

Eventually, since substance and primary qualities are thought of as real, and reality as only partially knowable, Locke is forced to appeal to a "deus ex machina" for a resolution of his difficulties. "The first are simple ideas, which since the mind, as has been shown, can by no means make to itself, must necessarily be the product of things operating on the mind, in a natural way, and producing therein

4. John Locke, *An Essay Concerning Human Understanding*, ed. A. C. Fraser (Oxford, 1894), Vol. I, Bk. ii, Chap. xii, Sections 1–3, pp. 48–49. All succeeding references will be to this edition and will be given in the text.

those perceptions which by the Wisdom and Will of our Maker they are ordained and adapted to. From whence it follows, that simple ideas are not fictions of our fancies, but the natural and regular productions of things without us, really operating upon us; and so carry with them all the conformity which is intended; or which our state requires . . ." (II.iv.iv.4;229).

In the third book of the *Essay*, Locke turns his attention to abstract ideas which do not have their source in the external perceptual world. He suggests here that the complex idea is actually an arbitrarily fixed collection of ideas, and that the objective validity can be insured only through the precise definition of general terms. Here we have the beginning of a theory of meaning which does, in fact, seem to be a cornerstone of the philosophy. "For, the connexion between the loose parts of those complex ideas being made by the mind, this union, which has no particular foundation in nature, would cease again, were there not something that did, as it were, hold it together, and keep the parts from scattering. Though therefore it be the mind that makes the collection, it is the name which is as it were the knot that ties them fast together" (II.iii.v.10;50). The universal is fixed by the precise definition that calls it into being, and the agreement that maintains it.

The fact that Locke devotes the whole of his third book to a study of the formation and use of the word indicates his recognition of the seminal position of language in the philosophy. But here again, he is unwilling to accept completely the implications of his reasoning. To build his epistemology around a theory of meaning would be to involve it in the kind of relative and subjective possibilities that he is anxious to avoid. To concentrate upon the composition of the nominal essence and the abstract universal is to deal with the peculiarities of the individual experience: the arbitrary definition of meaning. The chaos which might easily result from a subjective test of validity is parodied brilliantly by Sterne in the learned symposia of *Tristram Shandy*, the most noteworthy of which is found in "Slawkenbergius's Tale."

While Locke himself was obviously aware of the dangers inherent in this situation, his only alternative would have been the rigorous systematic analysis of language attempted by the analytic philosophers of our own time. Locke never develops his theory in this direction but, for the most part, insists that language, while essential to thought, is not to be identified with it. The concept is to some extent independent of the word and dependent for its existence upon the real essences from which sense perceptions are derived. This obviously returns him to the fundamental paradox with which he begins: the fruitless search for an incontrovertible truth hidden beneath relativity. This is the form of the quest undertaken by all of Sterne's heroes.

✤

Of equal importance to Sterne is another area of Locke's consideration of ideation: his attempt to come to terms with the unconscious aspects of the thought process. In the first edition of his *Essay*, Locke suggests that there may indeed be ideas in the memory which influence men's opinions and behavior, yet are not subject to the processes of the understanding. The "unnatural" connection of ideas suggested here apparently remained a disturbing problem for him, and in the fourth edition he added the section "Of the Association of Ideas." Although the suggestions included in this section offered many possibilities of a philosophical and psychological nature, none were developed systematically, and his general handling of the problem reflected great uncertainty as to the amount of emphasis to be placed upon the process of association, the degree of universality implied by it, and the tolerance to be extended to it.

The greatest stumbling block for those critics of Sterne who have considered the influence of Locke's theory on *Tristram Shandy* has been just this apparent contradiction inherent in Locke's presentation of association as both a dangerous deviation and an inevitable and universal mode of thought. The pivotal point of the difficulty is Locke's use of the word "madness" to characterize this function: "I shall be pardoned for calling it by so harsh a name as madness, when it is considered that opposition to reason deserves that name, and is really madness; and there is scarce a man so free from it, but that if he should always, on all occasions, argue or do as in some cases he constantly does, would not be thought fitter for Bedlam than civil conversation" (I.II.xxxiii.4;528). It becomes clear, however, from a close reading of this brief section of the *Essay*, that Locke's use of the pejorative term is motivated less by a desire for scientific accuracy than by his wish to impress upon the reader the serious implications of this sadly human propensity: "And if this be a weakness to which all men are so liable, if this be a taint which so universally infects mankind, the greater care should be taken to lay it open under its due name, thereby to excite the greater care in its prevention and cure" (I.ii.xxxiii.4;528). As Locke defines and re-defines this process, its universality is, in fact, increasingly accentuated, and the element of eccentricity is presented as the variable symptom of a complex and generally prevalent disease.

At first glance, Locke's basic definition of association would seem to allow of a very limited application: "Ideas that in themselves are not all of kin, come to be so united in some men's minds, that it is very hard to separate them; they always keep in company, and the one no sooner at any time comes into the understanding, but its associate appears with it; and if they are more than two which are thus united, the whole gang, always inseparable, show themselves together" (I.ii.xxxiii.5;529). Here Locke seems to be speaking of an accidental association which functions as memory, rather than of a synthesizing and creative process.[5] However, when Locke sets out to suggest some of the areas of men's lives which are governed by the tendency to associate ideas on the basis of private inclinations, education, and interests, we find implied a much broader interpretation of the process. Indeed, we find something which is related to the memory yet still akin to the subconscious—directing, forming, and changing all aspects of the individual's inner life. We learn, for example, that it is to these unnatural associations that "might justly be attributed most of the sympathies and antipathies observable in men" (I.ii.xxiii.7;530). To these associations are attributed also the contraction of all kinds of habits and defects (I.ii.xxxiii.17;539), as well as the formation of different sects of religious and philosophical thought (I.ii.xxxiii.18;534–35). Finally, Locke makes it clear that he cannot insist strongly enough upon the possible ill effects of wrongly conceived associations: "This wrong connexion in our minds of ideas in themselves loose and independent of one another, has such an influence, and is of so great force to set us awry in our actions, as well moral as natural, passions, reasonings, and notions themselves, that perhaps there is not any thing that deserves more to be looked after" (I.ii.xxxiii.9;249,531).

Locke still insists that "some of our ideas have a *natural* correspondence and connexion one with another: It is the office and excellency of our reason to trace these, and hold them together in that union and correspondence which is founded in their peculiar

---

5. See Arthur H. Cash, "The Lockean Psychology of *Tristram Shandy*," p. 127. This is the aspect of Locke's theory that Cash emphasizes.

beings" (I.II.xxxiii.5;529). But he does not explain which ideas would escape the infection of the unnatural associations that defy the attempts of analytic reasoning: "When this combination is settled, and while it lasts, it is not in the power of reason to help us, and relieve us from the effects of it. . . . And here we see the cause why time cures certain affections, which reason, though in the right, and allowed to do so, has not power over, nor is able against them to prevail with those who are apt to hearken to it in other cases" (I.II.xxxiii.13;532). Indeed, Locke's theory, totally considered, is not a limited and extraneous footnote to the epistemology. It is rather so inclusive, so broad in its implications (although tentative and undeveloped) that it leaves the way open for, and even suggests, those systematic positions maintained by Hume and Hartley.

In the theory of association Sterne found the greatest possibilities for suggesting the uniqueness of individual development within a context of universal conditioning. It opened to him a new area of characterization and suggested a radical technique which allowed freedom while affording an underlying, rational structure. First of all, Locke's adherence to the pleasure-pain principle, his belief that the will was motivated by "an uneasiness of the mind for want of some absent good" (I.II.xxi.31;333), which was, of necessity, defined in accordance with habitually determined associations, supported the theory of ruling passions. Sterne largely subscribed to this view. In considering man's way of coming to terms with his world, he accepted with Hume and Hartley (reaching his conclusions independently) the associational determinism that converted objective fact into psychological truth: "It is curious to observe the triumph of slight incidents over the mind:——What incredible weight they have in forming and governing our opinions, both of men and things, ——that trifles light as air, shall waft a belief into the soul, and plant it so immoveably within it,——that *EUCLID*'s demonstrations, could they be brought to batter it in breach, should not all have power to overthrow it" (IV.xxvii.322). Man, as systematic reasoner, is at the mercy of his hypotheses: "It is the nature of an hypothesis, when once a man has conceived it, that it assimilates everything to itself as proper nourishment; and, from the first moment of your begetting it, it generally grows the stronger by every thing you see, hear, read, or understand" (II.xix.151). And Walter Shandy stands, of course, as the prototype of all such rigorous thinkers in that

"... like all systematick reasoners, he would move both heaven and earth, and twist and torture everything in nature to support his hypothesis" (I.xix.53). According to Sterne's view, this associational determinism permeates every aspect of the individual's intellectual and emotional life.

But Sterne does not yield to the temptation of abandoning the integrity of the individual self to a mechanistic chain of conditioned response. He does not follow the path taken by Hume, who obliterates the distinction between thought and impression by submerging the conscious, mediating self in the simple attractions and repulsions of the associational process (thereby digging psychology's grave at the very place of its birth). Instead he insists, with Locke, upon the dominance of a reflective consciousness that orders the impressions and ideas which are the only constants of the individual's experience. "SELF is that conscious, thinking thing,—whatever substance made up of,—(whether spiritual or material, simple or compounded, it matters not)—which is sensible or conscious of pleasure and pain, capable of happiness or misery, and so is concerned for itself, as far as that consciousness extends" (I.II.xxvii.17;458–59). Locke, in his attempts to define the self as it moves among the given impressions of a constantly changing subjective world, seems to relate it closely to memory: "... whatever has the consciousness of present and past actions is the same person to whom they both belong" (I.II.xxvii.16; 458). Sterne follows him in suggesting this relationship and goes beyond to urge the psychological value of self-imposed recollection.

Thus, Tristram, in his search for identity, attempts to rise above the mechanism of his responses by ordering his impressions—attempting to trace them to their source, discovering in memory the unifying self that is the sum of its experiences. That Tristram is hindered at every point by the conditioning forces that propel him, even at the moment of his seeking to become master over them, is the tragi-comic paradox of the human dilemma. But the affirmation is posited in the attempt. It is true that the extreme eccentricity of the Shandys contributes to a sense of the simplicity of their characterizations. It is true also that Sterne's acceptance of a past that is always relatively accessible and his inability to differentiate among levels of consciousness place him in an intellectual milieu that predates systematic psychology. Nevertheless, his view of man as artist-in-process is a curiously contemporary one; and the psychological insights and resultant structuring of his novel are nothing short of prophetic.

✤

Throughout the novel it is Sterne's psychological and practical orientation which determines his creative interpretation of Locke's *Essay* and enables him to discover in it a simplified unity and validity. This is as true of Sterne's handling of the ethical and linguistic aspects of Locke's philosophy as of his treatment of Locke's theory of ideation. In Locke he faced the same problems again and again: a fundamental split in attitude which characterized much of the abstract thought of his day and which, he must have seen, was closely related to the thinking of the common men.

When Locke turned his attention from the way in which men think and know to the way in which they act and speak, his double vision of the relation of the personal and subjective to the absolute involved him in familiar paradoxes. Man as moral agent was beset by the same doubts, the same lack of authority, as intellectual man. He was, in short, thrown back upon himself. Just as he had been deprived of the innate ideas which brought him into harmony with the physical world, so also was he denied the innate moral principles which alone could unite the social and religious universes of behavior. He was the victim of his environment and his nature: "Nature, I confess, has put into man a desire of happiness and an aversion to misery: these indeed are innate practical principles which . . . do continue constantly to operate and influence all our action without ceasing" (I.i.ii.3;66–67). The combination of this relatively defined set of principles with the individual laws arrived at by the subjective processes of thought initiates a generally unpredictable and variable combination of attitudes mirrored in the variations found among different social and national groups (I.i.ii.6;69; I.i.ii.9; 72). Locke maintains that God has joined private virtue and public happiness (I.i.ii.6;69) in much the same way that he insists upon the metaphysical regulation of man's concepts to his requirements, but he is once again hard put to indicate the way in which this harmony is realized in practical activity. Involved in the infinite complications of the free-will and determinism dilemma, Locke finally rests his optimistic belief upon ad hoc principles which seem largely incompatible with the general trend of his thought.

On one side, then, we have a seemingly deterministic view that grows out of Locke's belief that ". . . all that is voluntary in our knowledge is the employing or withholding any of our *faculties* from this or that sort of objects, and a more or less accurate survey of them: but *they being employed, our will hath no power to determine the knowledge of the mind one way or another . . .*" (II.IV.xii.2;338). On the other side we have his faith in the mind's ability to suspend the execution and satisfaction of any of its desires, to be "at liberty to consider the objects of them, examine them on all sides, and weigh them with others" (I.II.xxi.48;344). Locke is confident that ". . . it is not a fault, but a perfection of our nature, to desire, will and set according to the last result of a fair examination" (I.II.xxi.48;344). He also reassures us that "the highest perfection of intellectual nature lies in a constant pursuit of true and solid happiness" (I.II.xxi.48;344). But he cannot indicate systematically the way in which the *will* to examine is to be produced, the way in which the understanding is to be causally connected to the springs of action. Locke's practical awareness of both the efficacy of the promised punishments and rewards of an after-life and the importance of the limiting pressures applied by social opinion vies with his faith in man's reason and ultimate perfectibility. His defeat before the traditional nemesis is only another example of the conflict that repeatedly calls his conclusions into question. The moral considerations do not raise new difficulties for him. They are still fundamentally the expression of an uneasy compromise between the absolutes of rationalism and the relativity of empiricism.[6]

This same compromise appears again in Book III, *On Words*, in which Locke justifies his analysis of the use of language: "When it is considered what a pudder is made about *essences*, and how much all sorts of knowledge, discourse and conversation are pestered and disordered by the careless and confused use and application of words, it will perhaps be thought worthwhile thoroughly to lay it open" (II.III.v.16;52–54). He intends his analysis to serve the cause of "truth, peace, and learning" by encouraging men to "reflect on their own use of language; and give them reason to suspect, that, since it is frequent for others, it may also be possible for them, to have sometimes very good and approved words in their mouths and writings, with very uncertain, little, or no signification" (II.III.v.16; 53–55). One of Locke's primary tasks was to lay open and correct

---

6. Robert Alter makes this point in his valuable essay *"Tristram Shandy and the Game of Love,"* p. 318.

those abuses of language which served as the subjects of satire for those writers in the tradition of learned wit: "Nevertheless, this artificial ignorance, and learned gibberish, prevailed mightily in these last ages, by the interest and artifice of those who found no easier way to that pitch of authority and dominion they have attained, than by amusing the men of business, or employing the ingenuous and idle in intricate disputes about unintelligible terms, and holding them perpetually entangled in that endless labyrinth. Besides, there is no such way to gain admittance, or give defence to strange and absurd doctrines, as to guard them round about with legions of obscure, doubtful, and undefined words" (II.III.vi.9;64).

Locke's discussion of the seven abuses of language and his description of its foremost abusers (II.III.x.1;122; II.III.x.22;140) undoubtedly provided Sterne with some valuable material for his satirical portraits. Locke is clearly at his best in his exposition of the imperfection of words. While he finds language reasonably manageable in civil discourse (for the practical purposes of conversation) he finds it considerably less efficient in dealing with the greater subtleties of philosophical argument. He places greatest confidence in those names that describe simple ideas, and his examples indicate that he has in mind here only ideas of sensation rather than those of reflection or sensation *and* reflection (II.III.ix.18;114). In order to remedy the imperfections and abuses of language, Locke urges perfect and exact definition when dealing with substances and mixed modes (II.III.xi.15;156; II.III.xi.19;158), so that clear and determinate ideas will always be affixed to words. He seems to presuppose, fallaciously, that general agreement with regard to a definition is really an indication of the validity of a proposition, and his apparent aim is to purify language to such a degree that it will no longer have a subjective reference.

Such "purity" of meaning is of course impossible for Sterne. He sees the personal fallacy as responsible for the use and interpretation of every word. He indicates repeatedly the way confusion can result from use of the most straightforward names. Puns, innuendoes, and double entendres transform the simple object, whose identity and characteristics would be similarly defined by all, into the causes of painful and inarticulate confusion. Emotions, predispositions, and personal conditioning make definition impossible. Ambiguities abound and, while they may reflect the imprecision of language itself, they are primarily the result of individual eccentricities.

Tristram's humorous attempts at definition serve always to underline the disparity between the explicit and the implied, the absolute and the relative. Tristram presents himself ironically as the ideal Lockean man whose responses are always rational. " 'Tis language unurbane,——and only befitting the man who cannot give clear and satisfactory accounts of things, or dive deep enough into the first causes of human ignorance and confusion" (II.ii.85). His use of language, however, indicates to what extent it is a tool for persuasion and amusement rather than for knowledge and illumination. At every point Sterne seems anxious to reduce philosophical discourse to the civil level, the abstract to the practical, the academically precise to the intuitively simple, and he does this not only because the dramatic interplay of his characters demands it, but also that he may reveal the absurdity of the theoretical. Locke's desire for definition, for the production of clear and determinate ideas, is revealed as another example of pedantic illusion. Thus, when Walter questions Trim after he has finished reciting his catechism, asking what he means by "honoring thy father and mother," Trim can reply only by describing the practical action which makes the abstract word meaningful to him: "Allowing them, an' please your honour, three halfpence a day out of my pay, when they grow old." And Yorick responds: "I honour thee more for it, Corporal Trim, than if thou hadst a hand in the *Talmud* itself" (V.xxxii.393).

Tristram himself points out the way in which definition can cause confusion and dissension in an area where intuition, if left alone, can create harmonious understanding. "All I contend for is, that I am not *obliged* to set out with a definition of what love is; and so long as I can go on with my story intelligibly, with the help of the word itself, without any other ideas to it, than what I have in common with the rest of the world, why should I differ from it a moment before the time?" (VI.xxxvii.469). The expediency inevitable in the use of value terms is illustrated by Tristram's description of one of Walter's predominant qualities: " 'Tis known by the name of perseverance in a good cause,——and of obstinacy in a bad one" (I.xvii.43).

The strange power of language is emphasized repeatedly, and the strain of nominalism which runs through Locke's analysis is carried to an extreme, translated into pragmatic terms, and found to be at the core of the chaos and confusion that pervade everyday life. While Tristram can discover in his past many reasons for his ineffectual eccentricities, one of the most basic is the misfortune of his name. His difficulties grow in some part from Walter's stubborn belief "That there was a strange kind of magick bias, which good or bad names, as he called them, irresistibly impress'd upon our characters and conduct" (I.xix.50). And the name, when it becomes part of the psychology of expectation, exerts a strong influence in its own right. It is itself the reality and the active cause. Names rather than things or ideas become the focal point of action and, because of the relativity to which they are subject, act as primary causes of disturbance. Man is the victim as well as the creator of his language.

Sterne also recognized the danger inherent in Locke's total optimism about the power of education and the positive role of the environment in controlling the understanding, developing rationality, and discouraging faulty patterns of association. To his mind, formalized theories of education share the illusion of all pedantry and academicism. Thus, Walter's progress with his *Tristrapædia* is at every point outstripped by the growth of the son for whose benefit it is being created; his theory of auxiliary verbs, the *sine qua non* of all knowledge, achieves such a degree of involution that it encourages the adoption of a formal language that is incapable of supporting meaning. Yorick, the truly educated and reasonable man, is rejected by the community that ironically finds his commonsense values too difficult to assimilate, and Trim, whose intuitive commonsense rationality raises him above his masters, has not been subject to the discipline of a formal education.

❧

In a general way, then, while Sterne frequently rejected Locke's tendency to compromise, the *Essay* was invaluable to him in the points of departure it suggested. Not least valuable was the divergence of Locke's practical observations from his abstract formulations. This dichotomy implied something profoundly significant about the philosopher and provided Sterne with a powerful intellectual and aesthetic tool. Tristram, the apparent author of the novel, is created in Locke's image, and all of the Shandys partake of the paradox embodied in his work. Their dilemma is always that of man trapped by the limitations of his perceptions, understanding, and environment, searching for the unconditioned, absolute truths of pure reason. Their tragedy lies in the infinite elusiveness of such truth, in the persistent mystery of the world, in the illusion of the word. The note of comic positivism is struck by their ignorance of defeat: the undaunted and marvelously human aspiration.

As the real author of *Tristram Shandy*, Sterne stands beyond this infinite chain of blind striving and, therefore, beyond Locke himself. Accepting the implications of the philosopher's scepticism, not bound by Locke's desire to fulfill the demands of a systematic and analytical epistemology, he urges the resolution which Locke avoids. Sterne begins with the human being that Locke defines: a human being isolated in his extreme individuality, conditioned by his own history, limited by the conventional language which is his primary tool, driven in his relationships by private concerns, with recourse only to the relative concepts which have no stable and positive authority. The only truth he can achieve is that gained through his own organization of the chaos of experiential fact. Its test lies in the concurrence of others who proceed always from points of view particularly their own. Tristram defines the problem when he says of Walter:

> The truth was, his road lay so very far on one side, from that wherein most men travelled,——that every object before him presented a face and section of itself to his eye, altogether different from the plane and elevation of it seen by the rest of mankind.——In other words, 'twas a different object,——and in course was differently considered:
> This is the true reason that my dear *Jenny* and I, as well as all the world besides us, have such eternal squabbles about nothing. (V.xxiv.382)

Upon this view is based the development of all of Sterne's characters —not only the major fictional characters, but also those academicians and obscure, specialized thinkers inherited from the tradition of learned wit. The eccentricities of each man require that his perceptions, his reflections, and his descriptions have a unique and essentially uncommunicable quality.

It follows from this that Sterne would take a much dimmer view of the possibilities and validity of the processes of generalization and abstraction than did Locke. Doubting the strength of man's powers of rationalization and emphasizing the relativity of perception and description, Sterne occupies a position closer to that of Berkeley and Hume. Their view is that abstract ideas do not actually exist, that the perception and the concept are, in fact, identical, and that the universal notion is nothing but the particular idea employed as a representative sign. This position is demonstrated by Sterne in Toby's and Trim's private and concretely practical interpretations of all abstract and general terms with which they come in contact. Similarly, Berkeley's view that a general word can be used without there being affixed to it a precise, determined idea is echoed in Toby's use of general terms which have been learned but have no specific content for him. Finally, in Walter's expert manipulations of abstractions to build elaborate superstructures ungrounded in any reality outside of his own mind and imagination, Sterne radically questions the validity of reason's complex concepts, gained through processes of abstraction and generalization. In short, Sterne accepts in *Tristram Shandy* a reduction of Locke's epistemology to a theory of meaning, with all of the relativity and scepticism that such an acceptance involves.

Sterne could quite easily have become involved in the kind of solipsism that Berkeley could not avoid, if he had not developed Locke's ethic in a new direction. It was one of the few times that he voiced an optimism equal to that of his master. Whereas Locke had placed his hope in man's power to reason, to form, and to act upon abstract principle, Sterne denies that the will to examine is commonly found, and indicates (in his characterization of Dr. Slop, for example) that the formal knowledge of moral principles can by no means insure their realization in action, nor does it even imply a valid understanding of such principles. Sterne postulates, rather, an innate sympathy similar to Hume's principle of imaginative empathy and Shaftesbury's belief in the individual's reflexive response to the qualities and actions of others. According to this view, the uncorrupted men of benevolence and good will (the Tobys and Trims) can intuit and respond to in others that which they cannot express or even fully understand themselves. This view frees the idea from the word and presents man as part of a natural and harmonious order. The cause of formal knowledge is not forwarded, but meaningful and ethical human relationships are made possible.

As for the possibilities of communication as such, Sterne does seem to offer one alternative to mute and inarticulate intuition. Accepting as positive the implied values of an empirical epistemology (the dependence upon individual impressions and awareness, upon association, memory, and imagination), he rejects explicitly

Locke's separation of wit and judgment: "I need not tell your worships, that this was done with so much cunning and artifice,——that the great *Locke*, who was seldom outwitted by false sounds,—— was nevertheless bubbled here. The cry, it seems, was so deep and solemn a one, and what with the help of great wigs, grave faces, and other implements of deceit, was rendered so general a one against the *poor wits* in this matter, that the philosopher himself was deceived by it,——it was his glory to free the world from the lumber of a thousand vulgar errors;——but this was not of the number . . ." (III.xx.202). Whereas Locke finds wit (the assembling of ideas in accordance with their superficial resemblances) and judgment (the rational separation of ideas) to be completely independent functions, frequently incompatible and seldom the gift of the same person, the former infinitely inferior to the latter, Sterne finds their differences to be merely apparent, their similarities essential: ". . . they are two operations differing from each other as wide as East is from West.——So, says Locke,——so are farting and hickuping, says I" (III.xx.193). Or, in a more serious, albeit still metaphorical vein:

> ——Here stands *wit*,——and there stands *judgment*, close beside it, just like the two knobbs I'm speaking of, upon the back of this self same chair on which I am sitting.
> ——You see, they are the highest and most ornamental part of its *frame*,——as wit and judgment are of *ours*,——and like them too, indubitably both made and fitted to go together, in order as we say in all such cases of duplicated embellishments, ——*to answer one another*. (III.xx.200–201)

While Sterne urges the complementary functioning of wit and judgment, he clearly celebrates wit throughout his novel.[7] His rejection of Locke's absolutes and his refusal to trust the powers of rationality naturally cause him to take a dim view of man's capacity to judge and, judging, to communicate his judgments. Tristram represents, in a sense, the man of natural wit who strives for judgment. The book he writes is a testimony to the hopelessness of his search, but it is also a testimony to the creative power, resourcefulness, and validity of his wit. Judgment can create order, but the order is false because of its selectivity. Only the wit, employing the imagination

---

7. Sterne's treatment of Locke's ethical theory is discussed above.

to perceive and metaphor to express, can capture and retain multiplicity, thereby dealing with the variety and chaos of the experienced world.

Well can Locke advocate the elimination of figurative speech from serious reflections, since ". . . all the artificial and figurative applications of words eloquence hath invented, are for nothing else but to insinuate wrong ideas, move the passions, and thereby mislead the judgment . . . they are certainly, in all discourses that pretend to inform or instruct, wholly to be avoided . . ." (II.iii.x.34;146). Walter Shandy shares his opinion: "The highest stretch of improvement a single word is capable of, is a high metaphor,——for which, in my opinion, the idea is generally the worse, and not the better . . ." (V.xlii.405). But, significantly, both resort to metaphorical language when attempting to elucidate their abstract ideas. Locke inevitably defines the pivotal words of his epistemology in pictorial terms. The mind, for example, is compared to a darkroom, an empty cabinet, a sheet of white paper. The understanding is described as a mirror and as the "mind's presence room" to which the sensations are admitted. Locke's propensity for figurative speech, in those very circumstances in which he would explicitly oppose it, must have represented for Sterne yet another example of the lapse between theory and practice.

Just as Sterne urges full recognition of the physical man (totally dependent upon his sensations), of the isolated man (whose eccentricities are of necessity defined by the individuality of his perceptions), of the human man (who has recourse to natural sympathies rather than formal constructs), so too does he joyously demand acceptance of the man of wit—of Tristram, who sees and describes the world in all of its symbolic ambiguity; not the essences sought by reason and judgment, but the appearances, the great systems of correspondences, gleaned by the imagination. In the Shandean world, which certainly partakes of the universal, words and objects are metaphors for one another. Ambiguity and confusion grow out of fluidity, but so also does knowledge. Admittedly, it is not the absolute knowledge to which Locke aspires, but it is, in a sense, more complete, for it includes and records lovingly, if ironically, his aspiration.

This is the major irony that Sterne learned from Locke: the irony of the theoretical philosopher whose dedication to the unambiguous involved him increasingly in a subjective and fallible humanity. If Locke, supreme among rational men, could fall, who then could resist temptation? And was the temptation—the temptation, after all, to aspire—not in its way heroic? In addition, all of the paradoxes of Locke's *Essay*, all of the self-contradictions that had to do with men's ways of knowing, communicating, and behaving, suggested thematic and dramatic possibilities that were relevant to Sterne's total ironic vision. Finally, Sterne's happy confidence in the power of wit, coupled with the satirist's voice of paradox learned from master practitioners, enabled him to construct a complex system of ironies that was as perfectly suggestive in its expression and form as it was ambiguous in its meaning.

From his astonishingly acute and creative reading of Locke's *Essay*, Sterne discovered a way of uniting the most salient features of Augustan satire with the most exciting possibilities of the novel.[8] D. W. Jefferson has written convincingly of the extent to which Sterne was influenced by those writers who were part of "the tradition of learned wit":[9] by the ironic evaluation of Erasmus' *Praise of Folly*, by the tremendous erudition of Burton's *Anatomy of Melancholy*, by the egotistical self-involvement of Montaigne's *Essays*, and, perhaps most of all, by Rabelais' joyous laughter in the face of the absurd, his commitment to spontaneity and freedom. Because of the particular philosophical perspective which he achieved through his reading of Locke, Sterne was strongly attracted to the rich paradoxes he found in the works of these writers—by their verbal and dialectical energies as well as by their satirical approach to all intellectual and social pretension. But because of his philosophical perspective Sterne found it necessary to place the social comment of traditional satire in a different context. The title of his work suggests the point at which he diverged from his predecessors. His apparent interest in Locke's personal psychology determined the direction he would follow. His emphasis is always upon the individual. He is concerned with Tristram's life and his opinions, and he sets out to demonstrate that opinions can only be understood as expressions of the personality and the experience of a particular man. For the literary form to be appropriate, it had to be more novelistic than satiric. It had to be radically psychological.

8. John Traugott and Melvyn New relate *Tristram Shandy* exclusively to the tradition of Augustan satire, dismissing the centrality, in Sterne's work, of character and action. In both cases the arguments result in extremely flawed and partial readings. The following discussion is offered as a refutation of their positions.

9. "*Tristram Shandy* and the Tradition of Learned Wit."

In conceiving and learning how best to manipulate Tristram, his intrusive narrator, Sterne was undoubtedly helped by those writers who had spoken in their own voices or through the agencies of fictionalized personae: Rabelais and Burton, Montaigne and Browne, Pope and Swift.[10] It was Swift, of course, who was most important,[11] for he was the first to use the fully characterized persona as the focal point of his work, as a means of creating its formal movement, its ironic paradoxes, and its most profound meanings. In Swift, as in others of the Augustans, Sterne discovered a new way of imposing unity upon traditional materials. He learned that irony, as a technical and philosophical approach, could be extended from a local rhetorical device to a dramatic technique. As such it opened up new possibilities of characterization and facilitated the expression of a total vision through sustained action. Swift's satires brilliantly emphasized for Sterne the potentialities of a rhetorical irony that could unify theme and structure in a dramatic statement of tragic intensity. His irony does not function according to a simple principle of inversion, for one cannot grasp Swift's own perception of truth merely by reversing the position taken by any of his personae. All of them are carefully and subtly characterized by the opinions they express, the rhetoric they use, and the way in which they interact with the reader.

But as useful as Swift's narrative technique must have been to Sterne, it did not prove appropriate for his purpose. Swift wished to create in his satires a single character defined in terms of a particular habit of mind. His argument is impressive in its intensity because its development is unilateral, its judgment pejorative and, in some ways, simplistic. Sterne's problem is less rigidly defined, his

---

10. Wayne C. Booth in "The Self-Conscious Narrator in Comic Fiction before *Tristram Shandy*," discusses at length Sterne's predecessors in the use of the intrusive narrator. See also Ronald Paulson, *Theme and Structure in Swift's* Tale of a Tub; Wayne C. Booth, *The Rhetoric of Fiction*; Donald Frame, *Montaigne's Discovery of Man*; Ian Watt, "The Ironic Tradition in Augustan Prose from Swift to Johnson."

11. It is Sterne's relation to Swift that provides New with the focus of his argument. He discovers a common adherence to Latitudinarian thought, a common belief in "a spirit of moderation and humility based on an acknowledgement of man's physical and intellectual limitations" (p. 107). He views Tristram as the target of Sterne's satire, similar to Swift's Tale Teller, adequate as Persona, serviceable as historian, but never developed as fictional character. His discussion addresses itself to a limited number of formal and thematic comparisons and sacrifices much of the novel's complex unity.

argument is cumulative and diffuse, his Tristram more complex because he is individuated and placed in positions of interaction.

Oddly enough, because Swift's tone is more bitter, his irony is ultimately less difficult and, perhaps, less effective. Swift plunges his reader into the dangerous waters of explicit statement and implied meaning, forcing him to identify with the narrator-guide as they move through a progressive and metaphorical redefinition of attitudes and values culminating in a final profound inversion. At some point along the way the reader is shocked into awareness, dissociates himself from the fanatical narrator, and identifies with the stinging condemnation of Swift. He is reborn into a conscious acceptance of the ironic meaning.

Sterne's reader follows a similar course, but he finds it more difficult to disentangle himself from the rhetoric since Sterne's attitude toward Tristram is not pejorative, but tolerant and sympathetic. The reader shares Tristram's problematical search for self-definition and must differentiate between the pose and the poseur, the public and the private selves, the pretentious and the valid. He is made to understand his own role as he participates in Tristram's weaknesses and shares his insights. He, with Tristram, is the worthy object of Sterne's criticism and sympathy. The relativity of values, the autonomy of the word, the psychological flux of time become intensely subjective experiences. He too is an outcast among outcasts in a society whose normative values grow out of the combat between the aspiration, the potentiality, and the limiting condition. Satire is balanced and finally absorbed by the sympathetic understanding which has as its subject, in Tristram, the nature of the creative imagination: the artist-hero who identifies himself as he creates, whose creation is an outgrowth of his search for identity.

Swift had, in effect, carried the traditional themes and techniques of learned satire to their furthest extreme. As satirist, Sterne occupied a more moderate position. But Sterne did not write principally as a satirist. Because of his interest in the psychology of the individual as he relates to himself and interacts with others, Sterne wrote as a novelist. The tradition of learned wit was important to his development because many of its elements fit into the dramatic structure which emerged from his reading of Locke's *Essay*. But these elements were always subordinated to the demands of another form. Whether Sterne set out to write a novel is a question which must remain unanswered. He seems to have been equally aware of the accomplishments of satirists and novelists and equally desirous of ironically implying, through his own work, their limitations. Significantly, however, the questions which he asked about the individual and his relation to society made him inevitably part of the novel tradition, and the form which he developed as a way of answering these questions (a form which made the novel's structure a metaphor of meaning and the story a metaphorical expression of the form) made him a revolutionary—and a prophet.

Two

The Stylistic Irony

The complex relationship shared by Sterne, Tristram, and the reader is a primary source of the novel's ambiguity. It is also the basic source of its brilliance. Sterne constructed this relationship so that it would allow him to comment ironically upon the possibilities of rhetorical and artistic expression. He conceived it in such a way that it would demonstrate the nearly insurmountable difficulties of communication while allowing him to surmount these difficulties himself by the power of his art.

Sterne plays three roles. As satirist he is concerned both with the forms of social thought and the patterns of social behavior. As psychological novelist he interests himself in the uniqueness of the individual's behavior and mode of communication. Finally, as philosopher he measures the reality against the ideal. The satirist ironically describes the "is" while implying the "ought to be." The psychologist offers his "why": the motivation, the cause, the compulsion. The philosopher undercuts both with a radical query: what are the limitations of men when compared to the limitations of man?

Tristram is Sterne's partial spokesman. His avowed purpose is to recount his own life and opinions. He addresses himself critically to the attitudes and eccentricities of society and, therefore, shares Sterne's satirical purpose. As autobiographer he is a character in Sterne's novel. As both social critic and man-as-artist in search of himself, as the exposer of false forms and the would-be creator of order, he is caught in the empiricist trap, sharing some of Sterne's insights and purposes, but without Sterne's perspective.

In a curious way, Tristram is a somewhat debased type of Locke, who stands for Sterne as an archetypal figure of misguided aspiration and doomed striving. He is a clear-eyed observer of compromised values and worthless achievements, and an ineffectual projector of a new system. As the man of unfettered wit dealing in superficial resemblances and startling paradoxes, Tristram judges always from a slightly false position. His promised "opinions" are not really opinions at all, but rather random impressions, bursts of insight in which serious meaning is hidden beneath the sharp turn of phrase, the unexpected pun, the unlooked-for metaphor. His mind balks before the complete formulation. He is fascinated by obscurity and ambiguity.

Similar qualities are exposed in Tristram's attempts to present his "life"—a truncated, haphazard, strangely Freudian autobiography which focuses upon prenatal influences and the traumatic experiences of early childhood. The conventional facts of his personal history seem as random as the opinions. Developing the psychological implications of Locke's epistemology, Sterne emphasizes the emotional response, the irrational motive, the eccentric but predictable effects of conditioning. The imagination orders its materials and, governed as it is by intuition, functions according to its own rules and creates its own odd patterns. Tristram, the man in search of knowledge, artist, satirist, and biographer, is always struggling with his own personal and intellectual limitations as well as his habitual mode of expression. He does, in a sense, become victimized by the novel he is writing.

By giving us a narrator whose unreliability is developed on various levels, Sterne creates an image of confusion, multiplicity, and contradiction, a sense of human illusion and self-deceit. There is, first of all, Tristram's own awareness of the division between himself as writer and himself as fictional character: ". . . was it not that my OPINIONS will be the death of me, I perceive I shall lead a fine life of it out of this self-same life of mine; or, in other words, shall lead a couple of fine lives together" (IV.xiii.286). The illusion of immediacy and veracity which is flawed by the division of roles is flawed still further by the fact that Tristram does not remain consistently on a single level of perception and explanation. His point of view varies. He speaks with changing degrees of intensity. His responses are at times emotional, at times intellectual, upon occasion sentimental, frequently ironic. When he reports events that do not impinge directly upon his own life, he does not always attempt to justify his knowledge but accepts without question the position of omniscient author. While it is possible to trace these inconsistencies to Sterne's failure to detach himself adequately from his persona,[1] they can also be seen, and are indeed felt, as an appropriate part of a generally eccentric personality.

Tristram's personal inconsistencies are a force for order because his major difficulty (that he is an unknown and undefined fragment of an unknowable and undefinable universe) allows for the subsumption of all paradox. Nor is it surprising that Tristram's work should partake of this same confusion—defying classification and eluding understanding. He is able neither to choose an image of himself suitable for presentation to the reader, nor to decide upon the aesthetic values he would like his work to embody. His art and his search for self-knowledge are mutually dependent: creation and discovery reciprocal conditions. In the empiricist's world, which has as its center the unique, eccentric, and flawed consciousness of each observer, there can be no absolutes. It is natural that Tristram see himself simultaneously as the careful master of his art and the pitiful victim of his circumstances. He can create the illusion of control. He can experiment with the techniques of art and the methods of self-analysis, but at every moment he is crossed by the ungovernable fact of multiplicity.

Tristram is the would-be historian, wrestling with objective fact and defeated by a welter of subjective impressions. "To sum up all; there are archives at every stage to be look'd into, and rolls, records, documents and endless genealogies, which justice ever and anon calls him back to stay the reading of:——In short, there is no end of it;——for my own part, I declare I have been at it these six weeks, making all the speed I possibly could,——and am not yet born:——I have just been able, and that's all, to tell you *when* it happen'd, but not *how*;——so that you see the thing is yet far from being accomplished" (I.xiv.37). The facts alone, signs of a rational and intelligible order, can testify to his reliability as a reporter, but there is always some other, more pressing truth that demands priority: "——But where am I going? these reflections croud in upon me ten pages at least too soon, and take up that time, which I ought to bestow upon facts" (VI.xxix.456). The truth is the total of the

---

1. This position is adopted by Henri Fluchère, *Laurence Sterne, de l'homme à l'oeuvre*; A. A. Mendilow, *Time and the Novel*; and B. H. Lehman, "Of Time, Personality and the Author: A Study of *Tristram Shandy*."

narrative consciousness that creates a background for the story. It represents the opinions, attitudes, memories, illusions, and aspirations of the mind. Tristram, telling the story of that part of himself which existed in the past, cannot be separated from the undigested conglomeration of experience that stands for the self constantly re-created in the present.

In one of his sermons, discussing the moral lesson to be derived from the "Parable of the Prodigal Son," Sterne provides us with a valuable aid to understanding his concept of Tristram's role: "Is it that we are like iron, and must first be heated before we can be wrought upon? Or, is the heart so in love with deceit, that where a true report will not reach it, we must cheat it with a fable, in order to come at truth?"[2] The narrative style of *Tristram Shandy* is devised as an attempt to make the reader more malleable by involving him in the ambiguities, indirections, and contradictions which represent the truth on its level of appearance. Tristram states his own purpose as frankly didactic and primarily moralistic: ". . . this self-same vile pruriency for fresh adventures in all things, has got so strongly into our habits and humours——that nothing but the gross and more carnal parts of a composition will go down:——The subtle hints and sly communications of science fly off, like spirits, upwards;——the heavy moral escapes downwards; and both the one and the other are as much lost to the world, as if they were still left in the bottom of the ink-horn" (I.xx.57). But Tristram's purpose is didactic in a much more limited sense than is Sterne's. The total effect of the novel (for the reader who has learned Tristram's lessons) grows out of an insightful philosophical statement which has been fully realized artistically. To some extent, the reader on whom Sterne must ultimately depend for recognition is one who has emerged with a developed sensibility and intelligence, one who has divorced himself in large part from the "Sir" and "Madam" who epitomize the petty evils and intellectual sterility of society. For each of our narrators, therefore, we are given a corresponding reader.

Tristram's reader has a definite physical reality. He is ordered to shut doors, leave the room, move the furniture, check sources and references, and reread a chapter which has not been sufficiently understood. The subjectivity of his aesthetic response is recognized

2. Laurence Sterne, "The Prodigal Son," in *The Sermons of Mr. Yorick*, III:227.

at the same time that various general motives are constantly being ascribed to him. He might be said to serve the important function of scapegoat. If the book is judged unfavorably, it must be because of his prejudices. If Tristram is accused of devoting his time to trivia, the fault is found to lie with his insatiable curiosity:

> I know there are readers in the world, as well as many other good people in it, who are no readers at all,——who find themselves ill at ease, unless they are let into the whole secret from first to last, of everything which concerns you.
>
> It is in pure compliance with this humour of theirs, and from a backwardness in my nature to disappoint any one soul living, that I have been so very particular already. (I.iv.7)

There can be no question as to the nature of the person with whom Tristram must cope. He is representative of the society which is harshly and satirically judged in Tristram's "opinions." He is representative of the imperceptive critic who is responsible for the uneasy path which Tristram must follow as a novelist. He is representative also of the unintentional but culpable offenders who, by the very nature of their own peculiarities and prejudices, have been the causes of Tristram's inabilities and eccentricities. "Sir" and "Madam" are the "unlearn'd reader" who, it is taken for granted, cannot recognize a reference to Rabelais (III.xxxvi.226). They are the unimaginative readers, interested in the mundane facts and decriptions of Tristram's Grand Tour (VII.ix.490). They are the completely egocentric readers who, with Tristram's mother, have only one point of reference against which to measure the world (V.xii.368).

Tristram is forever setting rhetorical traps for these unsuspecting victims. He carefully develops syllogistic propositions, the major terms of which are only partially clear. For example, when Dr. Slop describes the dangers of a forceps breech delivery to Walter, his hypothesis is not made explicit:

> ——What the possibility was, Dr. *Slop* whispered very low to my father, and then to my uncle *Toby*.——There is no such danger, continued he, with the head.——No, in truth, quoth my father,——but when your possibility has taken place at the hip,——you may as well take off the head too.
>
> ——It is morally impossible the reader should understand this,——'tis enough Dr. *Slop* understood it. . . . (III.xvii.188)

The reader's curiosity is stimulated but not directly satisfied. The fact that he can hardly help but understand the implications involves him in the guilt of the prurient. His position is made more difficult by Tristram's insistence that he pretend innocence before Walter's continuation of the proposition (his innocence is the same as ignorance and confusion) or admit to a sophistication which is synonymous with immorality.

In a similar way, Tristram frequently puts a false hypothesis into the reader's mouth, only to delight in undercutting it—as here, when the abstract hypothesis is opposed by the concrete fact, the relevance of which is purposefully obscure:

> You will imagine, Madam, that my uncle *Toby* had contracted all this from this very source;——that he had spent a great part of his time in converse with your sex. . . .
>   I wish I could say so,——for unless it was with her sister-in-law, my father's wife and my mother—my uncle *Toby* scarce exchanged three words with the sex in as many years;——no, he got it, Madam, by a blow. (I.xxi.67)

The reader's inability to understand what Tristram has deliberately made ambiguous and even paradoxical is presented as the chief cause of the novel's irregularities. It is also offered as an example of the kind of absurdity with which Tristram—the man as well as the artist—is constantly faced and by which he is continually frustrated. By involving the reader directly in the difficulties of ambiguous expression, Sterne is able to give immediacy to one of his major themes. However, because most of Tristram's method consists of a series of traps which are designed to force the reader into false responses, the real reader—Sterne's reader—becomes increasingly aware and therefore separable from his fictional surrogate. By developing a dramatic relationship between the narrator and the naïve reader, Sterne is able to play with the epistemological difficulties inherent in communication. As the "real" reader divorces himself from this relationship, he recognizes the extent to which Sterne has surmounted these difficulties through the force of his wit and art. To him, the ironic meaning is revealed. It lies beneath the surfaces of implication and ambiguity.

The rhetorical irony.—The syntactical structure of *Tristram Shandy* is carefully designed to support the intimate yet contentious relationship developed between naïve reader and narrator. Exploiting to its furthest limits the conversational tone used by earlier satirists and developed in the tradition of the continental novel, Sterne created for literature one of its outstanding works in the extravagant tradition of the "baroque." Morris Croll describes the tradition this way: "Its purpose is to express as far as may be, the order in which an idea presents itself, when it is first experienced. It begins, therefore, without premeditation, stating its idea in the first form that occurs: the second member is determined by the situation in which the mind finds itself after the first has been spoken, and so on throughout the period, each member being an emergency of the situation."[3] Formal techniques do not capture the immediacy and spontaneity of introspective thought or free conversation. What are needed instead are long complex sentences, the main clauses of which, while frequently connected by relative pronouns and subordinate conjunctions, often lack logical connection. This quite typical paragraph, which begins as an observation upon oaths and ends as a condemnation of critics, exemplifies the loose construction. Each clause is stimulated by the one preceding. There is a series of obscurely connected ideas, but not a cohesive argument.

> I'll undertake this moment to prove it to any man in the world, except to a connoisseur;——though I declare I object only to a connoisseur in swearing,——as I would to a connoisseur in painting, &c. &c. the whole set of 'em are so hung round and *befetish'd* with the bobs and trinkets of criticism,——or to drop my metaphor, which by the bye is a pity,—— for I have fetch'd it as far from the coast of *Guinea*;——their heads, Sir, are stuck so full of rules and compasses, and have that eternal propensity to apply them upon all occasions, that a work of genius had better go to the devil at once, than stand to be prick'd and tortured to death by 'em. (III.xii.180)

The advantage of this technique lies in the ease with which it conveys the immediacy and spontaneity of thought in process. Here, when Sterne speaks as an artist in search of himself, we are given the raw material which precedes the ordering of reflective processes. The emphasis lies not upon the truth of the proposition but upon

3. In his essay "The Baroque Style in Prose," Morris Croll discusses this anti-Ciceronian tendency that flourished between the high Renaissance and the eighteenth century (p. 446).

the essential realism of the psychological experience. The difficulties of such a technique are those which are imposed upon the reader who is forced to enter into a sympathetic, dramatic relationship with the narrator. He must share the experience of pre-conscious creation and must derive meaning from psychological insights as well as rational understanding. Nor is this the only rhetorical relationship that reader and narrator share, for Tristram, like Swift's narrator in *A Tale of a Tub*, is also a mock-baroque stylist, building elaborate structures that tremble or fall. Here again it is Sterne's reader who must fill in the gap between the meaning of Tristram's statement and the implication of his excessively artful rhetorical formulation. Tristram sets out to embroil and trap the reader, creating in him a new awareness of reality. The rhetorical figures designed to promote doubt, confusion, contradiction, and awareness of multiplicity also reveal similar states of mind in Tristram, who is frequently victimized by the form of his own work. In perspective, these structures comment about universal conditions of perception and interpretation: the illusory and problematical nature of experience.

It is one of Sterne's ironies that the rhetorical techniques which are customarily thought to implement logic and order should be used as the forms of chaos. Tristram's weakness for histrionics, revealed in his liberal use of apostrophe and invocation, places his honesty in a questionable light. His inability to follow consistently any protracted line of thought is demonstrated in his repeated use of aposiopesis and digression. Both of these figures pose particular difficulties for the reader: the first places upon him the burden of developing the implications of a thought or coping with a questionable innuendo, and the second deprives him of the security and grounding of a familiar, ordered plot. Similar effects are gained by harsh transitions, lengthy retrogressions and amplifications, constant corrections and revaluations. Further, asyndetons and catalogues tend to emphasize the similarity and diversity which are part of a complex multiplicity.

Serving a similar double-edged purpose is Sterne's use of the mock-heroic, not only to underline ironically the triviality of an event but also to stress the important role of personal perspective in interpreting the meaning and value of an incident. It becomes clear that the relative importance of every gesture or action must be acknowledged at the same time that its lack of absolute relevance is recognized. Thus, Uncle Toby's customary response to all that surprises, confuses, or appalls him is described thus: ". . . directing the buccinatory muscles along his cheeks, and the orbicular muscles around his lips to do their duty——he whistled *Lillabullero*" (III. vi.164). The exaggerated, mock-serious quality of the diction underlines the slightness of Toby's gesture, but also gives to it force of effort and earnestness of intention. The exorbitant rhetoric which Tristram employs in his description of the hot-chestnut incident serves the same dual purpose, for the attention paid to each small detail emphasizes the burlesque nature of the scene while it suggests the diners' love of argumentation and the crucial weight actually given to the absurd. It might be noted also that the quality of the description parallels the way in which the incident is to be made critical in Yorick's life (IV.xxvii.320–21).

In general, we find that Tristram's use of language represents a fascinating mixture of attitudes. At times he easily adopts the ready, ambiguous phrases of common usage. At other times he insists upon employing the closest scrutiny in choosing his word. Occasionally using language with complete unconcern for its nuances, he seems also to possess an almost poetic sensitivity. Frequently he will exhibit a contradictory attitude within the limited space of a single sentence, as he does when complete openness conflicts with close-mouthed prudery: ". . . he ordered his . . . cloak-bag to be brought in; then opening, and taking out of it, his crimson-satin breeches, with a silver-fringed——(appendage to them, which I dare not translate)——he puts his breeches, with his fringed cod-piece on . . . " (IV.249). It is impossible to identify with certainty the nature of Tristram's intention. Does this contradiction speak for Tristram's sly and ironic baiting of the reader, or does it merely suggest that, deep in concentration over the difficulties of translation, he inserts—carelessly—the very word which he has vowed to omit? Indeed, the emphasis which Tristram has placed upon the omission, and the matter-of-factness with which the remainder of the sentence proceeds, can easily cause the inattentive reader to remain oblivious to the paradox. This example is typical of the difficulties one encounters when attempting to differentiate between Tristram's own unconscious lapses and the limitations which he tries to impose upon the reader. From Sterne's perspective, of course, the differentiation is unimportant. It is by obscurity that his point is made. His skillful manipulation of syntax and language underlines both the interrelationship and the delusory nature of truth and the word. The

reader is made aware, despite himself, of the unavoidable dependence of language upon the intention, perspective, and technical
virtuosity of the man who speaks and the man who listens. The
reality of the problem is made more immediate by the fact that the
terms of the ironic equation are only suggested, never firmly defined, and no clear resolution is offered.

The result of the rhetorical method is to emphasize the universality and seriousness of the linguistic problem. Ultimately, the
only resolution that Tristram can find is escape from ordinary linguistic forms. He resorts to graphic signs in much the same way that
Trim, Walter, and Toby resort to wordless gestures in moments of
greatest frustration or deepest emotion.[4] The Shandean dash, which
indicates the rate of movement allowed to thought and feeling, the
italics which indicate emphasis, the black page introduced when
sorrow makes speech inadequate, the marbled page which is "a
motley emblem of my work!" (III.xxxvi.226), the diagram that indicates the relation of the digressions to the major segment of the
story, and the asterisks, physical signs of ambiguity—all these and
more are expressions of Tristram's defeat before the abstractions
and paradoxes of the verbal medium. They are the most extreme
forms of the intensely personal, impressionistic aspect of Sterne's
rhetoric.

But Sterne does offer an alternative to this extreme by the overall
example of his own technique. He accepted the synthesizing power
of the wit and the imagination in their creation of a private and
artistic order. He recognized, with philosophical resignation, that
communication involved each man in his own attempt to persuade,
not through reason but by his ability to surprise, shock, cajole, and
charm. He embraced, therefore, a rhetorical and syntactical form
which in itself implied disorder and confusion, and impressed the
reader with the force of its total effect rather than by the logic of
its argument or the neatness of its progression.

The chapter structure.—The distinction already made between Tris-

---

4. William V. Holtz, in *Image and Immortality: A Study of Tristram
Shandy*, relates Sterne's typographical oddities to the tradition of literary
pictorialism which, Holtz argues, had a substantial influence upon the author
of *Tristram Shandy* (pp. 80 ff.). Holtz's emphasis upon the pictorial effects of
the novel, and the thematic and technical implications of these effects, is
instructive, although extremely partial.

tram the novelist, victimized by his inability to sustain the form of his work, and Sterne the rhetorician, manipulating the reader in order to stimulate in him a new awareness of reality, is useful again when we attempt to define the novel's more general structural principles. Here we have Tristram the artist, determined by the associations and temporal relativity over which he can exercise no control, and Sterne the stylist, who uses the structure of his work to maximize dramatic and ironic effects.

It is not difficult to discover in the placement and juxtaposition of *Tristram Shandy*'s 312 chapters the duality of purpose and effect which is basic to the formal concept of the work.[5] Tristram, in his "chapter upon chapters," claims complete autonomy in this area of composition as he does in all others:

> ———A sudden impulse comes across me———drop the curtain, *Shandy*———I drop it———Strike a line here across the paper, *Tristram*———I strike it———and hey for a new chapter!
> The duce of any other rule have I to govern myself by in this affair———and if I had one———as I do all things out of all rule———I would twist it and tear it to pieces, and throw it into the fire when I had done———Am I warm? I am, and the cause demands it———a pretty story! is a man to follow rules——— or rules to follow him? (IV.x.281)

In actuality, there are firm logical principles determining the chapters.[6] It is only because there is more than one principle at work and because Sterne does not want to appear consistent that a feeling of disorder is created. Since Sterne's use of chapters is intrinsically bound up with the dramatic and dialectical relationship that he seeks to establish between Tristram and the reader, the feeling he is most anxious to stimulate is one of excited and involved confusion. Whenever the story threatens to proceed in a smoothly conventional way, he finds it necessary to introduce some element of surprise to disorient and mystify.

Tristram will frequently begin a chapter with a strong statement that contains an indefinite subject, the concrete nature of which is

---

5. Phillip Stevick briefly discusses the unconventional nature of Sterne's chapter structure in *The Chapter in Fiction: Theories of Narrative Division.*

6. For a closer analysis of Sterne's digressive technique see William Piper, *Laurence Sterne.*

revealed only after much extraneous comment, and the direct relevance of which can only be deduced from fragmentary information. Thus we have Tristram's introduction to the problem of the broken door-hinge obscurely following a rather long discussion of the relative merits of wit and judgment. He does not even bother, at first, to identify his subject: "Every day for at least ten years together did my father resolve to have it mended,——'tis not mended yet;——no family but ours would have borne with it an hour,——and what is most astonishing, there was not a subject in the world upon which my father was so eloquent, as upon that of door-hinges" (III.xxi. 203). It is typical of Tristram's technique that even the explicit identification of his subject does not clarify his intentions with regard to it. The role which the door-hinge plays as a force for disorder is revealed in the next chapter and at a later time in the novel, and its general importance as one of the insignificant objects of the Shandy world which wields an awful and unsuspected power can only be detected upon retrospective consideration. The momentary surprise is not conducive to a recognition of pattern.

Contributing to the same effect is Tristram's habit of beginning a chapter in the midst of an intense conversation which has no obvious connection with what has preceded it. The account of Walter's response to the breaking of his second son's nose is immediately followed by a heated if enigmatic argument between his great-grandfather and his great-grandmother concerning their marriage settlement:

CHAP. XXXI

——I think it a very unreasonable demand,——cried my great grandfather, twisting up the paper, and throwing it upon the table.——By this account, madam, you have but two thousand pounds fortune, and not a shilling more,——and you insist upon having three hundred pounds a year jointure for it.——

——"Because," replied my great grandmother, "you have little or no nose, Sir."—— (III.xxxi.217)

The unexpected nature of the conversation and the reader's ignorance of the circumstances surrounding it prevent him from making full connection between Walter's sorrow and the marriage settlement. It is only through a growing familiarity with the importance of noses in the Shandy "mythos," with its relation to the problem of impotence as considered on different but related levels, that this obscure association can be understood and Sterne's perspective shared.

Similarly, Tristram begins his chapter describing the visitation dinner in the middle of an impassioned debate (IV.xxvi.316), and then has to work his way out in all directions. Or he introduces Tristram's critical window sash accident with a statement that re-assures the reader about a situation of which he is totally ignorant. "——'Twas nothing,——I did not lose two drops of blood by it ——'twas not worth calling in a surgeon, had he lived next door to us—thousands suffer by choice, what I did by accident.——Doctor *Slop* made ten times more of it, than there was occasion:——some men rise, by the art of hanging great weights upon small wires,—— and I am this day (*August* the 10th, 1761) paying part of the price of this man's reputation" (V.xvii.376). Then, promising to explain why Toby must share with Trim and Susannah the responsibility for Tristram's unexpected circumcision, he begins as indirectly as possi-ble with a bit of dialogue between Trim and Toby about "mounting a couple of field pieces in the gorge of that new redoubt." Because it is so confusing the conversation serves to involve the reader more immediately than a simple and direct presentation of the fact (Trim's dismantling of the sash windows to forward Toby's campaign) could ever have done (V.xix.377).

Although Tristram occasionally ends his chapters or volumes with a conventional summary and statement of anticipation (IV.xxxii. 336–38; VIII.xxxv.593), it is most common for him to turn the transitional period to a specific dramatic purpose. Typically, the dialogue chapters will conclude upon a tense note in which clear division rather than violent antagonism is implied: a civilized com-pliance which is, in fact, disagreement. Thus the scene in which Walter laments Tristram's evil fate while Uncle Toby offers tenta-tive, optimistic reassurances concludes with a brief statement by each: "We will send for Mr. *Yorick*, said my uncle *Toby*.——You may send for whom you will, replied my father" (IV.xix.298). The finality of the rhythm, contrasting sharply with the baroque flow of Walter's earlier utterances, suggests at first a kind of truce or agreement but actually underlines the irrevocable separation of the two attitudes. A similar dramatic effect is achieved in another scene in which the ambiguities of speech are emphasized in the lack of mutual understanding which plagues all of Sterne's characters, as

well as the reader. Here, Doctor Slop and Toby reach a familiar
kind of impasse: "———Sir, replied Dr. *Slop*, it would astonish you
to know what Improvements we have made of late years in all
branches of obstetrical knowledge, but particularly in that one single
point of the safe and expeditious extraction of the *foetus*,———which
has received such lights, that, for my part (holding up his hands) I
declare I wonder how the world has———I wish, quoth my uncle
Toby, you had seen what prodigious armies we had in *Flanders*"
(II.xviii.144). Doctor Slop and Toby are left staring at one another
in disbelief as Tristram blandly begins his next chapter:

> I Have dropp'd the curtain over this scene for a minute,———
> to remind you of one thing,———and to inform you of another.
> (II.xix.144)

No attempt is made to clear up the confusion before the first chapter
of the next volume (a mere thirteen pages later), and even then the
attempt proves abortive.

Tristram's ironic stance is made still more ambiguous by the extent to which it emphasizes the unreliability of his narrative. There
are numerous examples of the self-defeating effect of the mock-
heroic tone:

> But whether that was the case or not the case;———or whether
> the snapping of my father's tobacco-pipe so critically, hap-
> pened thro' accident or anger,———will be seen in due time.
> (II.vi.101)
>
> . . .
>
> How my uncle *Toby* and Corporal *Trim* managed this matter,
> ———with the history of their campaigns, which were no way
> barren of events,———may make no uninteresting underplot in
> the epitasis and working up of this drama.———At present the
> scene must drop,———and change for the parlour fire-side.
> (II.v.99)
>
> . . .
>
> What business *Stevinus* had in this affair,———is the greatest
> problem of all;———it shall be solved,———but not in the next
> chapter. (II.x.108)

The pleasure that Tristram takes in exercising control over the
reader—his pompous, self-conscious, and barely disguised insistence
upon the mystery—combine to create a sense of uneasy distrust.

Beyond Tristram's conscious desire to involve and therefore instruct the reader, it is his involvement in a perverse system of causality and an obscure logical procedure which seems most relevant in the determination of structure and the placement of chapters. Tristram's story represents, in a sense, an infinite regression, for every occurrence, every meeting, every statement is revealed as an effect that holds the identity of its cause within itself. Tristram presents himself as a scientist, the would-be discoverer of first causes: "My way is ever to point out to the curious, different tracts of investigation, to come at the first springs of the events I tell . . ." (I.xxi.66). But there is a great disparity between his intention and his capacity ever to reach an understanding of the smallest causality. The more directly he strives for definition, the further he is carried away from his subject. Frequently Tristram will describe an incident, only to find it necessary to add later an account of its cause. Thus we learn that Toby is in a sudden hurry to leave Shandy Hall before we are told of Trim's project for him: a project to be executed in his own garden (II.v.93). At times, cause and effect will seem hopelessly entangled, as in the case of Uncle Toby's wound, his modesty, and the Widow Wadman's "concupiscence." Sometimes Tristram will omit, while ostensibly attempting to present his argument with clarity, an essential bit of information or a middle term which is necessary if the given conclusion is actually to be derived from the premise.

> The fact was this, That, in the latter end of *September*, 1717, which was the year before I was born, my mother having carried my father up to town much against the grain,——he peremptorily insisted upon the clause;——so that I was doom'd, by marriage articles, to have my nose squeez'd as flat to my face, as if the destinies had actually spun me without one.
>
> How this event came about,——and what a train of vexatious disappointments, in one stage or other of my life, have pursued me from the mere loss, or rather compression, of this one single member,——shall be laid before the reader all in due time (I.xv.41).

Tristram's dilemma is complex. It is also, to some extent, consciously imposed. He dramatically engages the reader in direct proportion to the befuddlement he causes him, and he is not above parodying his situation, trying in an openly playful way to ensnare

Sir or Madam. Here he begins with a faulty hypothesis: ". . . it seems strange, that Nature, who makes every thing so well to answer its destination, and seldom or never errs . . . should so eternally bungle it as she does, in making so simple a thing as a married man." He then offers a few explanations for the mysterious phenomenon, ending with a carelessly stated possibility ". . . that her Ladyship sometimes scarce knows what sort of a husband will do . . ." (IX.xxii.625–26). This undercuts everything that has preceded it.

Finally, there is a kind of diagrammatic realism and immediacy contributed by the unconventional use of structural devices. It is one of the ways, probably the most abstract, in which Sterne's work strives for and achieves artistic effects. Here the elusive thought and action which seem so chaotically conceived are given specific spatial positions. Their relationships can almost be physically grasped. This is true of the finality conveyed by the rhythm of Tristram's one-sentence chapters:

> My uncle *Toby*'s map is carried down into the kitchen. (IX.xxvii.638)
>
> . . .
>
> ——I'll put him, however, into breeches said my father,—— let the world say what it will. (VI.xv.433)

Here a graphic force contributes to succinct emphasis, as is true also of Tristram's insistence upon returning to chapters xvii and xix of his ninth volume—after having reached chapter xxv—in order to fill in the pages which he left blank (IX.xxv.632). The flashback is given an unusual immediacy, as the reader is made physically albeit deceptively aware of the writer writing, the book being written. Similarly, by merely implying the pivotal point of Toby's and the Widow Wadman's misunderstanding in IX.xx.623 ("——and where-abouts, dear Sir, quoth Mrs. *Wadman*, a little categorically, did you receive this sad blow?") and not making it explicit until IX.xxvi.638, Tristram gives one a concrete feeling of the suspense, frustration, and bewilderment experienced by the would-be lovers. And, finally, with this kind of chapter transition we have, vividly created, the crescendo movement of anticipation with the abrupt plunge of frustration:

> . . . then touching his under jaw with the thumb and fingers

of his right hand before he opened his mouth,——he delivered
his notion thus.

Chap. XXXIX

Just as the corporal was humming, to begin——in waddled
Dr. *Slop*. (V.xxxviii.400)

The complex network of chapters is manipulated expertly to
achieve the most subtle of ironic and dramatic effects which derive
their greatest strength from the ambiguity of Tristram's position.
The possibilities of every implication are multiplied by one's ignorance of the speaker's nature. The extent to which this narrative
technique (which seems to be at least partially self-defeating) is
actually essential to the realization of Sterne's purpose can be best
considered as it relates to Sterne's use of association as one of two
primary structural devices.

The association of ideas.—As shown in Part I, Sterne accepted the
broadest possible interpretation of Locke's theory of association.
It became for him a primary tool for delineating character and
creating structure. Those who have denied the overall importance
of association in *Tristram Shandy*[7] have not recognized the extent
to which Sterne expanded his definition in the direction previously
suggested in *An Essay Concerning Human Understanding*. He followed Locke in going beyond the traditional view of association as
the habitual reproduction of ideas experienced contiguously in the
past, and emphasized, rather, the importance of predisposition or
expectation in interpreting experience. As Tristram explains, describing Toby's misunderstanding of Walter's clearly ambiguous
question, "How goes it with your Asse?": ". . . our preconceptions
[have] (you know) as great a power over the sounds of words as
the shapes of things . . ." (VIII.xxxii.584–85). According to this
view, past associations—with their concomitant attitudes—determine
the individual's responses to new experiences.[8] Indeed, it can be said
that Sterne shared Hume's conviction that it was with the association

---

7. Arthur Cash, John Traugott, and Kenneth Maclean can all be included
in this category. Cash and Traugott find association to be important principally in the characterization of Uncle Toby, and Maclean recognizes it only
as a description of an extreme pathological state of which the Shandys are
representative.

8. Locke adopts this approach in the specific case histories he cites.

of ideas that the very framework of thought processes lay: ". . . the thought floated only in Dr. *Slop*'s mind, without sail or ballast to it, as a simple proposition; millions of which, as your worship knows, are every day swimming quietly in the middle of the thin juice of a man's understanding, without being carried backwards or forwards, till some little gusts of passion or interest drive them to one side" (III.ix.167). But he accepted, somewhat simplistically, Locke's pleasure-pain principle as fundamental cause and, relating this to the theory of ruling passions, developed his concept of character. It is the generality of Sterne's application of both the theory of the association and the theory of ruling passions that makes the Shandys as plausible and three-dimensional as they are. It is his intuitive sense of detail, his eye for the particular, his understanding of the vulnerability beneath the eccentric and stubborn response that make his concept more complex than it would at first seem.

The novel's digressive structure is based upon the directly experienced associations of Tristram the narrator and the associations of other characters which are recorded by Tristram and subordinated always to his own thought processes. Although this progression via association does not give the reader a sense of the general unity at any single point, it does make intelligible the local structure: the transition from one moment of action to another, from the situation, word, or gesture to the response, from the narrator's present to the digressive material. These associational responses take place on varying levels of sophistication. They provide the reader with basic insights into the characters and account as well for the novel's erratic form.

Throughout the novel there is a continual dependence upon the most simple and obvious form of association, the repeated contiguous occurrence of specific events, so that the presence of one will eventually call forth an expectation of the other: ". . . from an unhappy association of ideas which have no connection in nature, it so fell out at length, that my poor mother could never hear the said clock wound up,——but the thought of some other things unavoidably popp'd into her head,——& *vice versâ*:——which strange combination of ideas, the sagacious *Locke*, who certainly understood the nature of these things better than most men, affirms to have produced more wry actions than all other sources of prejudice whatsoever" (I.iv.9). We are offered a similar but more concrete juxtaposition to explain the Widow Wadman's attachment for Uncle

Toby, following his stay at her house: ". . . she can see him in no light without mixing something of her own goods and chattels along with him——till by reiterated acts of such combinations, he gets foisted into her inventory" (VIII.viii.546).

For Sterne, however, the process of association is always revelatory of far more than accidental temporal or physical contiguity. As a function of the total personality, it is indicative of a complex system of attitudes and values and therefore provides him with an excellent tool for ironic comment. For example, as part of the final tale of physical frustration and comic misunderstanding, we learn that Obadiah had brought his cow to mate with Walter's bull on his own wedding day.

> Therefore when *Obadiah*'s wife was brought to bed—*Obadiah* thanked God——
> ——Now, said *Obadiah*, I shall have a calf: so *Obadiah* went daily to visit his cow. (IX.xxxiii.646)

More than an example of association based upon the contiguity of events, Obadiah's response reflects the orientation of his mind and life, both of which are dedicated to the performance of duty rather than the satisfaction of personal appetites. His response is comic, as the unexpected tends to be, but there is also an undercurrent of the tragic which naturally accompanies an inversion of values: a sense of waste and futility.

Clearly there is implied by Sterne's treatment of association as an outgrowth of the ruling passions, a rudimentary theory of the subconscious which underscores the disparity between the individual's illusion of control and the actual unknown, anarchical darkness of the personality. Speaking of his father, Tristram observes that ". . . he had a thousand little sceptical notions of the comick kind to defend, ——most of which notions, I verily believe, at first enter'd upon the footing of mere whims, and of a *vive la Bagatelle*; and as such he would make merry with them for half an hour or so, and having sharpen'd his wit upon 'em, dismiss them till another day. . . . such guests . . . after a free and undisturbed entrance, for some years, into our brains,——at length claim a kind of settlement there,—— working sometimes like yeast;——but more generally after the manner of the gentle passion, beginning in jest,——but ending in downright earnest" (I.xix.53). The less complex the personality, the more intuitive the response. The less sophisticated the awareness, the less generalized and varied will be the articulation of the "ruling passion" in each individual and the less distinguishable will be the opinions from the "life" which engenders them. Thus, Walter's consciousness is the most inclusive, apart from Tristram's; his interests are, by definition, the most complex. His associations draw upon varied and unorthodox materials. He would subsume everything under a hypothesis, eliminating all that defies systematization. The disparity between his confidence in rational control and his actual obscurity and lack of sensible response mark him as the most deluded of the Shandys.

Uncle Toby, on the other hand, holds no real opinions. His own life is the direct source of all of his attitudes. His most obscure associations can be traced to his hobbyhorse, which reflects in its single-mindedness and innocence the totality of his personality. "Your sudden appearance, Dr. *Slop*, quoth my uncle, resuming the discourse, instantly brought *Stevinus* into my head. . . . Because, continued my uncle *Toby*, the celebrated sailing chariot, which belonged to Prince *Maurice*, and was of such wonderful contrivance and velocity, as to carry half a dozen people thirty *German* miles, in I don't know how few minutes,——was invented by *Stevinus*, that great mathematician and engineer" (II.xiv.116–17).

The way in which associations are indicative of the total orientation of the individual is nowhere more brilliantly demonstrated than in the "below-stairs" reception of the news of Bobby's death. The response of the foolish scullery maid is the simplest and most universal. Her associations give her little to draw upon. In her lack of sophistication she can refer only to a primitive sense of self: "——He is dead! said *Obadiah*,——he is certainly dead!——so am not I, said the foolish scullion" (V.vii.360). Obadiah, who is totally involved with his duties, recognizes immediately the practical implications of the event. Since Bobby's Grand Tour is no longer a possibility, the other alternative for the expenditure of his master's legacy has become a reality: "I heard the letter read with my own ears, answered *Obadiah*; and we shall have a terrible piece of work of it in stubbing the ox-moor" (V.vii.360). Susannah, whose romantic temperament and connection with ladies of higher rank have given her some desire for the accoutrements of social success, makes the most frivolous of associations and offers the most openly selfish response:

————My young master in *London* is dead! said *Obadiah*.——

————A green sattin night-gown of my mother's, which had been twice scoured, was the first idea which *Obadiah*'s exclamation brought into *Susannah*'s head.——well might *Locke* write a chapter upon the imperfections of words.——Then, quoth *Susannah*, we must all go into mourning.——But note a second time: the word *mourning*, notwithstanding *Susannah* made use of it herself——failed also of doing its office; it excited not one single idea, tinged either with grey or black,——all was green.——The green sattin night-gown hung there still.

——O! 'twill be the death of my poor mistress, cried *Susannah*.——My mother's whole wardrobe followed. (V.vii.359–60)

Most sophisticated and complex of all is Trim's response, an outgrowth of his military career and his connection with Walter Shandy. Trim offers an impassioned bit of oratory that is concerned with the dread mortality of man, and concludes with the most imaginative and eloquent of gestures."————'Are we not here now;'——continued the corporal, 'and are we not'——(dropping his hat plumb upon the ground——and pausing, before he pronounced the word)——'gone! in a moment?' " (V.vii. 362). With its mild philosophical abstractions, its warm humanity, and uncompromising, pragmatic recognition, Trim's brief sermon contrasts sharply with the historical compendium of unrelated musings upon death that Walter offers to assuage his own sorrow. The breadth of Walter's reading, his gift for expression, and the richness of his associations all provide him with uncommon resources, but value, commonsense, and intelligibility are lost in the profusion. It is with good reason that Tristram is moved to comment about his father's eloquence that ". . . it was indeed his strength——and his weakness too.——His strength——for he was by nature eloquent,——and his weakness ——for he was hourly a dupe to it; and provided an occasion in life would but permit him to shew his talents, or say either a wise thing, a witty, or a shrewd one . . . ——he had all he wanted.——A blessing which tied up my father's tongue, and a misfortune which set it loose with a good grace, were pretty equal . . ." (V.iii.352).

The "ruling passion," then, with its sister theory of association, is not at all a simple concept for Sterne. It takes into account the relative emotional and intellectual qualities of the individual: the

nature and variety of his experiences and the broadness of his interests. Sterne's characters, therefore, are not oversimplified as they
might seem at first. Using as a measure their capacity for absorbing,
organizing, and interpreting new experiences, Sterne places them on
an ascending scale that progresses from the total simplicity and egocentric reference of Mrs. Shandy, to the scullery maid, to Susannah
and Obadiah, to the naïveté of Toby and the Widow Wadman,[9] to
the commonsense perceptions of Trim and the perverse intellectuality
of Walter.[10]

It is true, of course, that the world in which the Shandys move is
limited, but these limitations are determined by Tristram within the
context of the novel. The characters are never allowed to stand
alone but are always presented clearly as forms of Tristram's
memory, part of the complex task which he has set for himself,
subject to the distractions of his vision. Thus, while Tristram is
telling the story of Toby's courtship of the Widow Wadman, we are
aware of him as the narrator but unaware of his specific temporal
and geographical position until he suddenly breaks off in the middle
of an elevated invocation to the "Gentle Spirit of sweetest humour,
who erst didst sit upon the easy pen of my beloved CERVANTES"
and begins barking orders at a hitherto unintroduced coachman:
"——Turn in hither, I beseech thee!——behold these breeches!——
they are all I have in the world——that piteous rent was given them
at *Lyons*——" (IX.xxiv.628). The reader is suddenly projected
into a totally new time and place, and Toby's amours are translated
into a state of the narrator's mind: "I was in the most perfect state
of bounty and good will; and felt the kindliest harmony vibrating
within me . . ." (IX.xxiv.629). In a similar fashion, Tristram can
blithely abandon his father to his bed of grief, leave Mrs. Shandy
guiltily hidden behind a door, or keep Walter and Toby breathlessly
poised upon the staircase.

Standing for Sterne as the narrating consciousness, Tristram is
unique in the extent to which his mind is explored and the totality
of his experience is presented. He is, in a sense, more complete than
any of the other characters; his associations are made on a more

9. Although it is the Widow Wadman's concupiscence which is most frequently mentioned as her most outstanding quality, this is (as we shall see)
only the naïve expression of a perfectly normal concern that suffers by its
comparison with the abnormal constraints of others of her class.

10. Yorick is not included here since he serves a peculiar function in the
novel, standing somewhere outside of the action as a chorus character whose
comment introduces an element of balance and perspective.

conscious level. He seems to be less a victim of his instincts and intuitions, although his whole investigation bears testimony to the fact that he is conditioned by his environment. This paradox is due to the somewhat contradictory nature of the roles he plays as narrator and character in his own novel. Tristram is the autobiographer-novelist who remembers in order to understand himself. Demonstrating the Lockean relation of identity with memory, he proceeds unconsciously as artist and eccentric, haphazardly piecing together those fragments of his life which are inextricably bound up with the lives closest to his own. But insofar as Tristram is simultaneously satirist and philosopher, he is self-conscious—actively commenting and editing. If he has not been in control of those events which have made him what he is, he does control, to some extent, his view of these events. He is ironically aware in a way that none of the other Shandys are allowed to be.

But this ambiguity does not detract from the validity of his associations, nor does it invalidate the claim that *Tristram Shandy* is the first of the stream-of-consciousness novels.[11] It is true that Tristram's associations cover an unusually broad field, existing on an intellectual as well as an emotional level. Tristram shares Walter's love of trivia, of oratory, of the obscure, but his interest is turned both inward and outward. He is aware and unaware, conscious and unconscious. Like Leopold Bloom, he does at times initiate thought, attempting to pattern and rationalize; at other times his mind is a passive receptacle for loosely associated ideas, vaguely recalled memories, disjointed scraps of information and impressions. His hobbyhorse is defined by the book he writes. It is as wide-ranging and complex as that book, and it is for this reason that Tristram is in some respects the most completely realized of the Shandys—"in some respects" because he is also the most elusive.

Tristram's ambiguity as a character derives primarily from his problematical relation to Sterne and is a function of Sterne's inability (or perhaps his lack of desire) to divorce himself completely from his persona. But it is also an essential concomitant of the novel's thematic and technical development. If the reader had been allowed to experience Tristram as a totally integrated character, the premises of Sterne's philosophical system would necessarily have been called

---

11. Henri Fluchère denies that *Tristram Shandy* is an "interior monologue" or "stream-of-consciousness" novel, because Tristram functions on a conscious rather than subconscious or unconscious level (p. 258).

into question. Tristram is only another aspect of the reader's complex, empirically defined universe. He can be intuited. He can be placed within a personal, subjective pattern of meaning. But he cannot be comprehended in all of his variety, his eccentricity, his uniqueness.

Duration.—The complexity of Tristram's role, the variety of his references, the fact that most of the personal experiences he describes are drawn from his gestation, infancy, and early childhood, while his responses and opinions seem to exist on a level apart from the immediately experienced: all of this detracts from one's sense of Tristram as a fully defined individual. It contributes also to his own self-alienation. He suffers from his immersion in the relativity of time. His life, deprived of strict chronological order, appears strangely gapped. From this point of view, all biography is psychological in nature and all must confront, at some point, the problem of duration.

In his book *Time in Literature*, Hans Meyerhoff has written, "Time is particularly significant to man because it is inseparable from the concept of the self. We are conscious of our own organic and psychological growth in time. . . . The question, what is man, therefore invariably refers to the question of what is time. The quest for a clarification of the self leads to a recherche du temps perdu, and the more seriously human beings become engaged in this quest, the more they become preoccupied and concerned with the consciousness of time and its meaning for human life" (p. 2). Sterne's interest in the mechanism of association led logically to his experimentation with a form that is a simplified version of the stream-of-consciousness technique. With his absorption in the problem of identity and in the related function of memory came the necessity of manipulating the temporal dimensions of his work in such a way as to emphasize the timelessness of the self: its continual endurance in the present through the eternal availability of the experiences by which it has been defined. Tristram is not fully realized because the combination of memories and opinions which he offers does not compose a cohesive, deeply conceived personality. There is no pattern discernible in our discovery of Tristram. His past self is not revealed in successively retrogressive and inclusive stages in the manner of contemporary stream-of-consciousness heroes. Tristram remains essentially the same throughout the novel. It is, in effect, the reader's attitude that changes—and this not so much because of his increased understanding of Tristram as because of his growing perception of the relationship established between the narrative perspectives of Tristram and Sterne. Sterne remained fascinated by the flexibility and mutual dependence of time and the self. An examination of the functioning of Tristram's mind in specific disparate areas served as a tool in his explorations of this flexibility. The definition of Tristram's personality was never more than a secondary goal. For all of his inventiveness, his fine penchant for eccentricity, Sterne was preoccupied with epistemological principles which could claim some universal validity and which would remain basically stable despite the wide variation of individual articulation.

As the most recent critics of Sterne have recognized, it was Locke's view of the relation of identity and duration that provided Sterne with his fundamental theory of time. Fewer have recognized the superior sophistication and insight of Sterne's interpretation. Locke chose to represent the thought process metaphorically as a "train of ideas." He suggested that the idea of succession was derived from our reflection on this "train of ideas," while the idea of duration was the result of our ability to distinguish between any two ideas or parts of the chain of succession. For him, the concept of duration was closely connected to the concept of space, with temporal intervals varying in accordance with the liveliness of the subject's mental activity and the intensity of his sensory stimulation. However, Locke did not elaborate upon or analyze the nature of the changes taking place in an individual's sense of time or the variations that would exist among any given group of individuals, but rather emphasized his conviction that the rate of succession remained relatively constant in all men.[12] His concept, which made no attempt to investigate systematically the possible relationship between the train of ideas and the phenomenon of association, remained essentially undeveloped.

Sterne's explicit treatment of Locke's theory of duration and his own resolution of problems of temporality raised new questions. For example, the different ways in which Toby and Walter deal with Locke's theory of the succession of ideas indicate the extent to which

12. Jean-Paul Sallé does, in fact, suggest that Sterne's concept of duration stands as a direct contradiction of Locke's and was actually derived from an observation of Addison's in *Spectator* 18 (June 1811), no. 94. See Sallé, "A Source of Sterne's Concept of Time," pp. 180–81.

their states of receptivity are diametrically opposed: "Now, whether we observe it or no, continued my father, in every sound man's head, there is a regular succession of ideas of one sort or other, which follow each other in train just like————A train of artillery? said my uncle *Toby.*————A train of a fiddle stick!————quoth my father, ————which follow and succeed one another in our minds at certain distances, just like the images in the inside of a lanthorn turned round by the heat of a candle.————I declare, quoth my uncle *Toby,* mine are like a smoak-jack.————Then, brother *Toby,* I have nothing more to say to you upon the subject, said my father" (III.xviii.190–91). For Tristram, who must correlate the multiple temporal levels on which reader, narrator, and characters function, the assumption of Locke's position represents the epitome of stylish scholastic sophistication. As always, Toby stands as a refutation of the formalized abstraction—proclaiming, by the fact of his being, the unknown quantity of the eccentric and the individual. Similarly, the complex mechanism of the novel's technique belies the simplicity of Tristram's own position. Problems of the reality and relativity of time, the role of the individual consciousness and imagination, and the interdependence and reflexivity of past and present (all of which are overlooked by Locke) are dealt with by Sterne in a sophisticated manner prophetic of Bergson.

As in all problematical aspects of *Tristram Shandy,* it is essential to distinguish between Sterne's position and Tristram's when attempting to pinpoint the novel's orientation. The error most frequently committed by critics of Locke's theory of duration involves an identification of Tristram's extreme, realist intentions with Sterne's own clearly defined purpose. Kenneth Maclean maintains this erroneous position: ". . . It was Sterne's prodigious intention to make his novel temporally realistic to the minute by providing the reader with one hour's reading for every waking hour in the life of his hero, a program he completed with considerable care and success—thru the first day. . . . The first day of Tristram's life ends on page 260, which 260 pages would conceivably take one day to pass as a succession of ideas through the reader's mind. According to this schedule it would have required 94,900 pages to cover a single year of Tristram's existence."[13] Actually, Tristram blunders into his paradox

13. *John Locke and English Literature of the Eighteenth Century,* p. 87. Lodwick Hartley, *This Is Lorence,* p. 85, and Watt, *The Rise of the Novel,* p. 292, among others, concur with Maclean on this issue.

because Sterne recognizes the logically absurd end which must ultimately be faced by the philosophical realist. His recognition anticipates the contradictions inherent in the method of contemporary realist novels and philosophy.[14]

In deciding upon the time-locus of his work—the temporal relationship of reader, writer, and hero, and the connection between chronological and psychological time—Sterne could choose among a variety of possible combinations. Because of his empiricist position he did not look upon the manipulation of temporal perspectives as a technical problem alone. It represented one of his key themes, central to his concern with the way in which the individual develops and communicates. The intensely subjective nature of every man's world, his isolation and frustration, could to a large extent be found to depend upon the intensely subjective nature of the time value which provided the basic medium of his thought. The constant clash of temporal levels is symptomatic of a universal predicament that permeates every area of one's intellectual, emotional, and imaginative life. Reader, writer, narrator, and characters all move in temporal universes of their own making and remembering. Thus it is Toby's emotional life which can be said to determine *his* durée while Walter's intellectual life conditions *his* sense of time. The time-values of writing, reading, and living are found to be strangely incommensurate, and all of Tristram's efforts at reconciliation do not heighten the realistic effects, but rather emphasize the futility of *his* attempt. The gap that exists between "private time" and "public time" cannot be bridged by reason and is penetrable only by intuition. Although Tristram offers a number of securely fixed signposts in the form of specific dates, these are found to stand upon a ground of quicksand. Once incorporated into the character's associational framework, the precisely worked out chronology becomes an expression of his own distorted, private perspective. Indeed, Toby and Trim's peculiarly idiosyncratic war games, which always adhere closely to specific dates and historical fact, express thematically this perverse relationship of chronological and empirical time.

Sterne's liberal use of the "time-shift" technique is extremely effective on a number of levels. A. A. Mendilow has appreciatively

14. Watt points out in *The Rise of the Novel* that Bertrand Russell in his *Principles of Mathematics* "modelled his own statement of the problematical nature of Time on *Tristram Shandy* and named his paradox after Sterne's infinitely regressive hero" (p. 293).

noted that "Sterne—'the laughing philosopher of English fiction'—continually breaks tenuous threads of his story—by way of some apparently irrelevant digression—enters on an illuminating comparison of different senses of time as it operates in the mind of the reader, author and characters he's writing about. . . . The yardstick is not the length or shortness of time but the swiftness or slowness of their sense of its passage. His counterpointing of these varying values makes Sterne the supreme virtuoso of the English novel" (p. 130). It is principally through the conversations among his characters, the comments of his narrator, and the use of interrelating digressions that Sterne creates successfully in the reader an acute awareness of the flexibility of temporal values.[15] The fluidity of movement, which his digressive structure allows, enables him to investigate at will the associations of his characters, to contrast and control his most extreme effects, to build to a climax, to a suspenseful pause, to a moment of complex recognition achieved from the consolidation of a number of seemingly disparate but obscurely related incidents. The temporal perspective is lengthened or abruptly telescoped, as when Tristram's associations cause him to bring together his visit to Auxerre as a child touring with his father and his uncle, and his stop in Auxerre as a man in flight from death. ". . . I am this moment walking across the market-place of *Auxerre* with my father and my uncle *Toby*, in our way back to dinner——and I am this moment also entering *Lyons* with my post-chaise broke into a thousand pieces—and I am moreover this moment in a handsome pavillion built by *Pringello*, upon the banks of the *Garonne*, which Mons. *Sligniac* has lent me, and where I now sit rhapsodizing all these affairs" (VII.xxviii.516).

Tristram's insistence that his own present—the writer's present—be carefully noted acts implicitly as a reminder of the contrasting presents of the actual writer, Sterne, and the reader. The most meticulously presented "truth" becomes a half-truth when it is viewed against the total perspective. Traugott is correct in seeing this as the primary irony of Sterne's time-scheme: ". . . the time-scheme of the book is that it is without sense of time, since events are an amplification of Tristram's opinion and of his characters, not a revelation of plot, and the characters do not change. The whole is always before us, and since Sterne insists upon the reader's participation in

15. Mendilow, pp. 132–33.

almost every line, we have the perfect irony of a view of the whole, including ourselves" (p. 43). But this irony and the broader irony of the novel's total structure are nothing if not elusive. A basic difficulty lies in the fact that Sterne's work does not follow a single structural principle. The mercurial narrator in search of himself, the digressive story development, the complex time-values, the Locke-inspired theory of association are distinct but interdependent principles which formally and thematically represent epistemological and artistic possibilities: ways of interpreting, knowing, and teaching. All indirectly emphasize the basic tension that exists between the universe of the imagination and the universe of reason.

The book which Sterne writes is not the same as the book which Tristram is writing. Tristram's logic becomes nonsense when the perspective is enlarged and, paradoxically, his nonsense reveals a strange kind of logic. The formlessness of Tristram's thought is the carefully planned outgrowth of Sterne's structuring, which does itself depend upon a number of principles, each of which can be mistakenly viewed as independent and dominant.

Because of the reader's involvement with the narrator, he is made aware of technique as subject. It is part of Sterne's genius that this obscure relationship of method and theme should be given a valid, objective reality. Tristram's writing is a function of his questioning. Tristram is himself a function of Sterne's inquiry and a tool of his ironic perception. The insightful reader who can differentiate one from the other while bearing in mind the fact that Sterne, with his philosopher's awareness of ambiguity, does not have the philosopher's need of ultimate solutions, is invited to watch from an objective and enlightened distance the play in which he is himself a player. It is not surprising that such a role would require a substantial amount of practice. It is indeed questionable whether Sterne, with his love of paradox, believed that the role could ever be perfected.

Three

The Thematic Irony

The formal technique of *Tristram Shandy* rests essentially upon a radical opposition and synthesis of surface and substance, deriving its strength from the separation of Tristram from Sterne. As we have seen, Sterne's art is characterized by its seeming artlessness. Its organization derives from the careful construction of confusion. Because of the attention which it devotes to its own process, *Tristram Shandy* is largely a novel about language and technique. If language is essential to communication, it is also an unfailing creator of misunderstanding. And rhetoric, which is, in a sense, language developed to its fullest potential, becomes the most effective instrument of deceit, hypocrisy, and ignorance.

But despite the fact that the novel's narrative discontinuity hinders our grasp of the work, an intelligible unity does in fact exist. It emerges from Sterne's manipulation of the novel's dominant themes, each of which is discussed with and realized through its negating opposite: sense of self and lack of identity, reality and illusion, sentimentality and irony, reason and emotion, language and gesture, sexuality and impotence, art and nature, creativity and death, the tragic and the comic. It is the interrelationship of these themes and the basic clarity of thematic conception that makes art of eccentricity.

The Irony of Character

Tristram Shandy is a novel of ideas. Its form is part of the idea, not a background for it, and the characters themselves are aspects of the intellectual quest, all constructed from some pivotal irony, subject to some central paradox, treated with sceptical insight as well as love. That is not to say that Sterne's people are two-dimensional representatives of specific positions, spokesmen for the successive stages of a dialectical formula, as Traugott would have it. They inhabit their personalities quite fully, although it is true that their personalities are limited by the uncompromising points of view from which they perceive the world. We watch them interpreting, acting, interacting, responding. Their realities meet, clash, and destroy one another, yet remain curiously intact, for each character has a basic integrity, a core of inflexible ego that keeps him unique and self-sufficient.

The odd way in which Sterne related the particular and the abstract (the irreducible human quality and far-reaching universal propensities) began in his pre-Shandean sermons, for it must be remembered that the man of letters had his birth in the man of God. Sterne's later sermons (the earlier sermons, published last, are primarily exercises in borrowing) reveal the author's persistent attempts to discover the motives of men's actions, the basic elements of personality and character. Lansing Van Der Heyden Hammond points this out in his book *Laurence Sterne's "Sermons of Mr. Yorick"*: "Time and again throughout the *Sermons* he reverts, obviously with the best of intentions, to the tenet that morality alone is insufficient as a motivating factor in human behavior—but invariably the naturalistic implications, not the teleological, are the ones he lingers over and illustrates" (p. 95). As a minister Sterne had surprisingly little interest in theological matters or traditional questions of doctrine. He was a moral philosopher who was concerned with the social effects of action rather than with their supernatural sanctions. As Hammond wrote, it was Sterne's desire to emphasize "the less striking, homelier virtues which count for so much in everyday living: toleration and kindliness, patience and understanding, thoughtfulness and sympathy, modesty and sincerity" (p. 96). These are also the saving virtues of the otherwise perverse characters of *Tristram Shandy*.

It is not surprising, therefore, although it is certainly unconventional, that Sterne would elaborate upon and even distort the texts upon which his sermons were based. When he could not find what he wanted in his text, he had no difficulty in composing a new one for his use. For example, when he deals with "The Character of Herod," he explains: "With this view, it may not be an unacceptable application of the remaining part of a discourse upon this day, to give

you a sketch of the character of Herod, not as drawn from scripture,
—for in general it furnishes us with few materials for such descriptions. . . ."[1] Similarly, in his sermon "The Levite and His Concubine," Sterne does not make use of the whole Biblical story which
ends with the Levite's surrender and subsequent dismemberment of
his concubine. He uses only the first half of his source, paradoxically
demonstrating with it the importance of courtesy and mercy: "It
serves no purpose to pursue the story further; the catastrophe is
horrid: and would lead us beyond the particular purpose for which
I have enlarged upon this much of it,—and that is, to discredit rash
judgement, and illustrate from the manner of conducting this drama,
the courtesy which the *dramatis personae* of every other piece, may
have a right to."[2] In general, when we compare Sterne's sermons
with the sources given us in Hammond's appendix, we find that
Sterne tends to concretize the generalization by relating every point
of view to a particular personality. Whenever possible, he adopts a
dramatic form of narrative, changing his own voice and implicating
his audience with an explicit address or direct quotation. As Traugott suggests, the result of his technique is the involvement of the
reader in a dialectic which emphasizes the crucial role of interpretation in differentiating the hidden truth from the obvious illusion.
This was to be used with great effect in the novel.

In "The Prodigal Son," which is typical of the mature sermons,
Sterne muses upon the father's attempts to dissuade his son from
undertaking his journey, describes sentimentally the emotional moment of departure, comments liberally upon the youth's impulsive
foolishness, elaborates upon his repentant thoughts as he entreats
Heaven to help him, and offers with great relish both a detailed
account of the boy's lapses into sin and an ironic description of the
falsity of the world. Rejecting more conventional discussions of the
parable, Sterne concludes with some up-to-date comments of his own
about the Grand Tour and its educational values. The sermon seems
quite prophetic of *Tristram Shandy* in that it bears the strong imprint
of Sterne's personality with his propensity for the dramatic and digressive, his sharp ear for dialogue, his desire to surprise through
jarring eccentricities of style and deft portrayals of emotional states,
his basically secular, practical orientation, and his marvelous sense
of the absurd and incongruous.

1. "The Character of Herod," in *The Sermons of Mr. Yorick*, I:105.
2. *Sermons*, I:211.

Of course, the didactic purpose of the sermons demanded a relative simplicity of structure and characterization. The concept of a "ruling passion" was particularly useful since it enabled Sterne to draw his moral issues clearly, centering motive and consequence upon a single peculiarity of character to which a definite value could be assigned. Using the "obsessions" of his major figures as the focal points of his sermons, Sterne was able to satisfy simultaneously the dramatic and moral demands of his work. Thus, in analyzing Herod, who is driven by "ambition, an immoderate thirst, as well as jealousy of power," Sterne explains his method of illuminating the character of his hero: "The way to which is—in all judgments of this kind, to distinguish and carry in your eye, the principal and ruling passion which leads the character—and separate that, from the other parts of it,—and then take notice, how far his other qualities, good and bad, are brought to serve and support that."[3]

This view of character, which had its roots in Locke's associationism, required a more sophisticated application in the complex situations and ideas of *Tristram Shandy*. In the Shandean world Sterne no longer had defined signposts by which to steer. Although his moral, artistic, and intellectual values might have remained fundamentally the same, they now had to function and validate themselves in a universe of constantly changing perspectives. Given free rein in the disorderly world of secular activity, the hobbyhorse—a concrete expression of the ruling passion—became a more unruly and complexly defined beast than Tristram himself suggests. "For my hobby-horse, if you recollect a little, is no way a vicious beast; he has scarce one hair or lineament of the ass about him——'Tis the sporting little filly-folly which carries you out for the present hour——a maggot, a butterfly, a picture, a fiddle-stick——an uncle *Toby*'s siege, or an *any thing*, which a man makes a shift to get astride on, to canter it away from the cares and solicitudes of life . . ." (VIII.xxxi.584). The hobbyhorse is a serious matter—as serious, Sterne reveals with great insight, as a child's game. It is both a function and an implied criticism of the romantic impulse. It is an expression of the urge to create value and an expression of the urge to sublimate or escape the limiting conditions of the actual. It is the illusion that lends importance to life by interpreting and re-creating reality. It reflects both the strength and the weakness of its possessor,

3. "The Character of Herod," p. 107.

derived as it is from his abilities and directed toward his aspirations. Thus Tristram does not exaggerate when he says " 'Tis as useful a beast as is in the whole creation—nor do I really see how the world could do without it" (VIII.xxxi.584). It is either with less insight or greater irony that he comments earlier that ". . . so long as a man rides his HOBBY-HORSE peaceably and quietly along the King's highway, and neither compels you or me to get up behind him,——pray, Sir, what have either you or I to do with it?" (I.vii.13). Indeed, one of *Tristram Shandy*'s primary themes has to do with the inevitable entanglement of hobbyhorses, with the rider's insistence that everyone should get up behind him. It is the thoroughness of the individual's involvement, the intensity of his commitment, that makes conflict unavoidable. And while the collision among riders disturbs the smoothness of the journey, it also prevents one from venturing too far from the common path.

In *Tristram Shandy*, then, the hobbyhorse becomes the focal point of the total personality. It connects the world of thought with the world of action and reveals the central irony of each character. The emergent ironic patterns, expressive of the disparity between aspiration and realization, are compared with one another to create a total picture of the perverse and abortive course followed by human relationships.

To consider these patterns in more detail, it is convenient to identify two distinct groups of characters: the first distinguished by its members' rationality, sophistication, and rhetorical finesse, the second by the individual's reliance upon intuition and sensibility. Walter, Tristram, and Yorick will, of course, be found in the first group; Toby, Trim, the Widow Wadman and Mrs. Shandy are in the second.

Walter Shandy.—Of all the Shandys, Walter's commitment to rationalism is the most extreme and explicit. He believes firmly in the mind's capacity for discovering, creating, and verbalizing truths which can lay claim to some objective validity. He is the scholar whose hobbyhorse (the creation of systems, the formalization of knowledge) is born from his attempts at reconciling the pure world of mind with a physical world that is volatile and full of contradiction. Walter's curiosity is endless. His love of the obscure and secret analogy, the unsuspected and surprising unity hidden in the physical object or the suggestive word, is insatiable and indiscriminate: "Then

reach me my breeches off the chair, said my father to *Susannah*——
There is not a moment's time to dress you, Sir, cried *Susannah*——
the child is as black in the face as my——As your, what? said my
father, for like all orators, he was a dear searcher into comparisons . . ." (IV.xiv.287). Yorick's opinion of Walter's insights can
be defended: ". . . there was a seasoning of wisdom unaccountably
mixed up with his strangest whims, and he had sometimes such illu-
minations in the darkest of his eclipses, as almost attoned for them:
——be wary, Sir, when you imitate him" (V.xlii.404). But Tristram's judgment is more generally applicable: "My father . . . [forced]
every event in nature into an hypothesis, by which means never man
crucified TRUTH at the rate he did . . ." (IX.xxxii.644). It is, of
course, the irony of Walter's position that his confidence in reason's
resources encourages the creation of imaginative illusions and leads
him to formulations that are altogether at variance with precepts of
commonsense.

Paralleling Walter's paradoxical faith in the absolute power of
reason and the eccentric and amateurish way in which he exercises
his faculty is the almost magical control he attributes to the word
and the affective, rather than analytic, possibilities which he inevitably explores in his own rhetoric. He believed "That there was a
strange kind of magick bias, which good or bad names, as he called
them, irresistibly impress'd upon our characters and conduct" (I.xix.
50). Here we find one of those problems which Locke had encoun-
tered: with what validity can one hypothesize a fixed core of
meaning that is somehow separable from the relativity of a word's
contextual definition and implication? Walter's suspicion of the name
"Tristram" arises partially from ignorance. He considers the name's
proper derivation, but he recollects erroneously the nature of the
men who had answered to it historically by overlooking the great
medieval hero who bore it: ". . . he says there never was a great or
heroic action performed since the world began by one called *Tristram*——nay he will have it, *Trim*, that a man can neither be
learned, or wise, or brave . . ." (IV.xviii.295).

It is precisely because of Walter's attitude that Tristram's name
comes to exert an influence upon the boy's conduct and character.
Sterne knew what Locke felt but would not accept: that language,
when considered in a psychological context, could assume a frightening life and power of its own. While it held great promise as the tool
of social intercourse, the implementation and perhaps basis of man's

ability to reason, its rich potentialities concealed many traps. Of these, Walter is frequently a victim. He is presented as a practitioner of language, a rhetorician, an orator: "He was certainly irresistible, both in his orations and disputations;——he was born an orator; ——Theodidaktos.——Persuasion hung upon his lips, and the elements of Logick and Rhetorick were so blended up in him,——and, withall, he had so shrewd a guess at the weaknesses and passions of his respondent,——that NATURE might have stood up and said, ——"This man is eloquent" (I.xix.51–2). But Walter's skill is intuitive, not conscious or rational: ". . . it was a matter of just wonder . . . that a man who knew not so much as the names of his tools, should be able to work after that fashion with 'em" (I.xix.53). Thus we have the paradox of the scholar or academician whose oratory springs from an intuitive ability and has an emotional appeal, but is no more based upon reason than are his fanciful systems, the children of a fertile and eccentric imagination. For Walter, argument is a game in which substance is made subordinate to method. It involves the assumption and acting out of various roles, as in his disagreement with Mrs. Shandy about the attendance of a midwife at the birth of his second child, "when he had done arguing the matter with her as a Christian, and came to argue it over again with her as a philosopher . . ." (II.xix.146). Walter's love of language— indeed, his addiction to forms of expression—is carried to its extreme and paradoxical end with his theory of the auxiliary verb, a parody of Aristotle's ten categories. Walter rejects the metaphor, prize of wit and imagination, the *sine qua non* of his own technique. Instead he suggests: "Now the use of the *Auxiliaries* is, at once to set the soul a going by herself upon the materials as they are brought her; and by the versability of this great engine, round which they are twisted, to open new tracts of enquiry, and make every idea engender millions" (V.xlii.405). The word, therefore, becomes father to the idea and restricts and determines the form of reality.

This odd impracticality, the ironic result of an attempt to achieve accuracy of thought and expression, is only one example of the conflict between the theoretical and the practical that frustrates and typifies Walter's life. His concoction of grandiose, abstract theories is linked most frequently to an inability to understand and control his own motivations and actions. Thus, his concern for money and reputation, in addition to a more honorable interest in the well-being of his family, motivates his opposition to his wife's confinement in the city. It is not surprising that he would rationalize his motives, but his rationalization is resourceful beyond any reasonable expectation. He attributes his refusal to a fear that the state would eventually collapse as a result of the movement of men and money to the city. And even here his altruism is brought into question as he expresses his concern for the demise of the squirearchy (I.xviii.47). Any matter that piques his intellectual curiosity causes him to sacrifice the concrete requirements of his family to the more abstract delights of the mind. He gleefully plays a practical joke on Dr. Slop, revealing the fit forms of swearing by having Slop read a form of the excommunication of the Roman Church. Meanwhile his wife lies in bed, awaiting the doctor's obstetrical services (III.xi.171–79). Similarly, Walter becomes immediately and passionately involved in the pedantic foolishness of the visitation dinner and forgets that he has come in order to change Tristram's name, the retention of which, he feels, invites certain doom (IV.xxix.326). He is a man with well-developed opinions about door hinges, but he has never bothered to oil that one which is an eternal problem to him, although ". . . three drops of oyl with a feather, and a smart stroke of a hammer, had saved his honour for ever" (III.xxi.203). How then can we or Mrs. Shandy be surprised when, hearing from Obadiah the news of his son's circumcision, he returns from a hurried trip upstairs, not with bandages and medicine, but with *Spencer de Legibus Hebræorum Ritualibus* and *Maimonides* (V.xxvii.384).

This unusual conflict between abstract interests and practical concerns frequently expresses itself in a dichotomy of emotion and reason—the most dehumanizing aspect of Walter's character. One is disquieted by Walter's blithe inquiry: "What is the character of a family to an hypothesis? . . . Nay, if you come to that——What is the life of a family . . ." (I.xxi.69). Involved as he is in the excitement of his own ideas, he is able to see his wife only as an object, a piece of personal property whose functions, abilities, interests, and life itself are defined as they relate to him. "It is very strange . . . that my wife should persist . . . in trusting the life of my child . . . to the ignorance of an old woman;——and not only the life of my child, brother,——but her own life, and with it the lives of all the children I might, peradventure, have begot out of her hereafter" (II.vi.99–100).

Walter's responses to incidents which would induce in most people a paroxysm of grief are the deformed offspring of a strangely incongruous and divided spirit. They indicate the extent to which Walter's hobbyhorse is a self-defeating attempt to construct for himself a meaningful reality that bridges isolation and frustration. The funeral oration "My Father's Lamentation" (a compendium of classical mourning literature) in response to Bobby's death, the rhetorical exercise presented on thè occasion of Tristram's unexpected circumcision, and his expression of grief by the assumption of a stylized posture when he learns of the crushing of his younger son's nose— all convey Walter's attempts to counter the unexpected and impersonal thrusts of fate with the only controls at his disposal, those of gesture and language. The man seems frequently to disappear behind his contrivance, and it is only rarely that we are allowed to glimpse the emotion that defies formalization. One of these moments is given to us in the image of Walter beside his brother's grave, perceived, presumably, by a more mature Tristram and recalled, therefore, with a fuller degree of consciousness and understanding. "——Where ——All my father's systems shall be baffled by his sorrows; and, in spight of his philosophy, I shall behold him, as he inspects the lackered plate, twice taking his spectacles from off his nose, to wipe away the dew which nature has shed upon them——When I see him cast in the rosemary with an air of disconsolation, which cries through my ears,——O *Toby*! In what corner of the world shall I seek thy fellow?" (VI.xxv.452). Less directly, we are left to detect the strains of emotionality that fairly scream through the intensity of Walter's intellectual attacks and belie the nature of his involvement:

> My father had such a skirmishing, cutting kind of a slashing way with him in his disputations, thrusting and ripping, and giving every one a stroke to remember him by in his turn—— that if there were twenty people in company——in less than half an hour he was sure to have every one of 'em against him.
>
> What did not a little contribute to leave him thus without an ally, was, that if there was any one post more untenable than the rest, he would be sure to throw himself into it. . . . (VIII.xxxiv.588)

Walter is ruled by his fear of spontaneity—a fear that is ironic in a man whose richness of imagination and intensity of spirit do, in fact, militate against the coldness and formality of a purely rational approach. In moments of greatest crisis the numbed philosopher is able to summon expressive forms which give him an illusory sense of controlling the uncontrollable reality. It is before the more ordinary circumstances of his relationships that the defenses crumble and his humanity is exhibited in all of its glorious illogicality and inadequacy.

The consistency of Walter's characterization and the piteousness of his circumstances are most fully revealed through his sexual conflict. It is in the physical functioning of man that Walter finds the most frightening signs of his own vulnerability and the most unhappy possibilities of spontaneous response. Walter's attempts to formalize the spontaneous inevitably end in failure and the attempt changes not only his life, but also the lives of his descendants. Indeed, Tristram's unfortunate fate is largely linked to his father's attitude toward sexuality, which is, one feels, only partially determined by the incapacities of age: "As a small specimen of this extreme exactness of his, to which he was in truth a slave,——he had made it a rule for many years of his life,——on the first *Sunday night* of every month throughout the whole year,——as certain as ever the *Sunday night* came,——to wind up a large house-clock which we had standing upon the back-stairs head, with his own hands:——and being somewhere between fifty and sixty years of age . . . he had likewise gradually brought some other little family concernments to the same period, in order, as he would often say to my uncle *Toby*, to get them all out of the way at one time, and be no more plagued and pester'd with them the rest of the month" (I.iv.8).

The repressive nature of the Shandys' sexual relationships is the ultimate expression of their inability to relate to one another: ". . . cursed luck! said he, biting his lip as he shut the door,——for a man to be master of one of the finest chains of reasoning in nature, ——and have a wife at the same time with such a head-piece, that he cannot hang up a single inference within side of it, to save his soul from destruction" (II.xix.147). But, more than this, Walter's final, bitter repudiation of the sexual act reveals its importance to him as an instance of the natural, spontaneous, and emotional elements in man which prove his animality and balance his spiritual and rational aspirations. "——That provision should be made for continuing the race of so great, so exalted and godlike a Being as man——I am far from denying——but philosophy speaks freely of every thing; and therefore I still think and do maintain it to be a pity, that it should be done by means of a passion which bends down the faculties, and turns all the wisdom, contemplations, and operations of the soul backwards——a passion, my dear, continued my father, addressing himself to my mother, which couples and equals wise men with fools, and makes us come out of caverns and hiding-places more like satyrs and four-footed beasts than men" (IX.xxxiii. 644–45).

It is, then, his refusal to recognize the needs of his own nature, and his inability to reconcile the practical demands of a contradictory, obscure, and frequently illogical world with the strivings of his soul and mind, that make of Walter a tragi-comic figure. Tristram's plea is well-founded: "Will not the gentle reader pity my father from his soul?——to see an orderly and well-disposed gentleman, who tho' singular,——yet inoffensive in his notions,——so played upon in them by cross purposes;——to look down upon the stage, and see him baffled and overthrown in all his little systems and wishes; to behold a train of events perpetually falling out against him, and in so critical and cruel a way, as if they had purposely been plann'd and pointed against him, merely to insult his speculations" (I.xix. 55–56). But still, while Walter seems doomed to suffer all the agonies of a cruelly impervious fate, his suffering is actually the absurd result of his absurdly limited vision. The unfortunate incidents which fill his life—as slight as the misnaming of one of his sons, as important as the death of the other—are all equally diminished by the nature of the consciousness which defines them. It is rather his isolation that achieves a tragic dimension: an isolation that grows from the disparity (we are reminded again of Locke) between the forms of his aspiration and the materials of the empirical world. The individuality of his experience alienates him both from himself—natural functions divided against vain strivings—and from others, who are also unique and also lonely.

Tristram.—In Tristram, Sterne gives us a new version of the paradox that plagues Walter. The father's fascination with processes of thought becomes in the son a preoccupation with the functioning of wit. Both would control and make meaningful the forms of reality with their particular methods of perception and expression. Both are defeated by the subjective limitations of imagination. On the level of action and communication they are rendered impotent.

Tristram makes it quite clear, at the well-known opening of his story, that his physical and intellectual endowments were thoughtlessly determined at the very moment of his conception: "I wish either my father or my mother, or indeed both of them, as they were in duty both equally bound to it, had minded what they were about when they begot me; had they duly consider'd how much depended upon what they were then doing;——that not only the production of a rational Being was concern'd in it, but that possibly the happy formation and temperature of his body, perhaps his genius and the very cast of his mind;——and, for aught they knew to the contrary, even the fortunes of his whole house might take their turn from the humours and dispositions which were then uppermost . . ." (I.i.4). As if the absurdity of his begetting were not a sufficiently negative force in the determination of his life, Tristram goes on to describe himself as a fool of Fortune, whose life has been filled not with great evils but with "pitiful misadventures and cross accidents" (I.v.10). It is with the descriptions of these misfortunes and accidents that the first six volumes are primarily concerned.

It must be noted, however, that Tristram's version of the catastrophic circumstances of his conception rests upon a favored theory of his father. Similarly, the effect on his life of the small misfortunes and accidents which are treated as critical milestones in his development can be largely attributed to passionate attitudes, communicated passionately to him. In short, it is in the subtly created relationship of the father to the son that we find the real roots of Tristram's own development.

Walter's beliefs and aspirations are determining factors, not because they have reference to a validating reality, but because they become in themselves versions of reality, positive causes of action. Nowhere is this clearer or more important than in the influence of Walter's name theory upon Tristram's life: its determination of the limits of Tristram's aspirations and the ironic forms of his failure. Trismegistus is the name that Walter carefully chooses for his son. Tristram is the name the child is mistakenly given. "But, of all the names in the universe, he had the most unconquerable aversion for TRISTRAM;——he had the lowest and most contemptible opinion of it of anything in the world——thinking it could possibly produce nothing in *rerum naturâ*, but what was extreamly mean and pitiful . . ." (I.xix.55). It is toward Trismegistus, the Egyptian god of fertility, inventor of writing, creator of language, reckoner of time, that the youngest of the Shandy males must eternally strive.[4] Like

4. M. K. Singleton, in his essay "Trismegistic Tenor and Vehicle in Sterne's *Tristram Shandy*," relates (albeit not very persuasively) *Tristram Shandy* to Greek and Latin Trismegistic or Hermetic Literature.

Sisyphus, he will come repeatedly within a hair's breadth of success, only to meet defeat—as Tristram: his life molded by the name chosen but not given, molded by Walter's prenatal expectations and postpartum disappointment. But, as with Sisyphus, the absurdity of his situation will contain within it the seeds of an ironic success that is part, not of the result, but of the effort.

Tristram does recognize, to some extent, the strength of Walter's influence upon him. For example, when he speaks of the muddle into which he has gotten both the reader and himself while trying to unify the diverse parts of his story, he explains: "——But 'tis my father's fault; and whenever my brains come to be dissected, you will perceive, without spectacles, that he has left a large uneven thread, as you sometimes see in an unsaleable piece of cambrick, running along the whole length of the web, and so untowardly, you cannot so much as cut out a ** . . . or a fillet, or a thumb-stall, but it is seen or felt—— (VI.xxxiii.462–63). Like Walter, Tristram is not attracted to an idea because of its relevance. The smallest association is sufficient to stimulate him and, once stimulated, he is engrossed by the possibilities for its development. Thus, after he presents Locke's explanation of the failure of the understanding to retain impressions and illustrates it in the little scene involving Dolly and the sealing wax, he acknowledges: "Now you must understand that not one of these was the true cause of the confusion in my uncle *Toby*'s discourse; and it is for that very reason I enlarge upon them so long, after the manner of great physiologists,——to shew the world what it did *not* arise from" (II.ii.86). Although Tristram is able to view his father's obsessive love of systematizing with some degree of objectivity and is clearly unwilling to go to the same extremes in his intellectual commitments, he is unable to resist the lure of an original hypothesis. Speaking of his father's views on swearing, he says: "The hypothesis is, like most of my father's, singular and ingenious too;——nor have I any objection to it, but that it overturns my own . . ." (III.xii.183). In the course of the book he does put forth many hypotheses of his own. They are concerned with such diverse matters as the inability of wit or judgment to develop in a northern climate (III.xx.196), the cyclical movements of history, with special emphasis on epistemological and cultural areas (I.xxi.64–65), and the advisability of using goat's whey as a cure for impotence and milk coffee to treat consumption (VII.xxx.518).

In general, there is a basic difference between the attitudes of father and son toward themselves, which determines the nature of their intellectual postures. The difference is one of perspective and imagination. While Tristram does share his father's eccentric interests, he is drawn always to the element of wit that is involved in the composition of an idea, rather than to the ramifications of the metaphysical exercise. "I am not such a bigot to *Slawkenbergius*, as my father;——there is a fund in him, no doubt; but in my opinion, the best, I don't say the most profitable, but the most amusing part of *Hafen Slawkenbergius*, is his tales,——and considering he was a *German*, many of them told not without fancy . . ." (III.xlii. 241). Tristram's acute interest in the possibilities of wit grows from his recognition of relativity as a dominant principle in the subjective universe. This recognition prevents him from committing himself absolutely to any statement or judgment. Like Walter, he delights in setting up a proof that will support a particular hypothesis; but, unlike his father, he is able to discover afterward without difficulty or upset that his hypothesis is somehow irrelevant to the proof (I.xxi.65). Further, this recognition of relativity is closely linked to his poetic and sentimental awareness of the transitory nature of work, life, and love: "Time wastes too fast: every letter I trace tells me with what rapidity Life follows my pen; the days and hours of it, more precious, my dear *Jenny*! than the rubies about thy neck, are flying over our heads like light clouds of a windy day, never to return more——every thing presses on——whilst thou art twisting that lock,——see! it grows grey; and every time I kiss thy hand to bid adieu, and every absence which follows it, are preludes to that eternal separation which we are shortly to make" (IX.viii.610–11).

If Tristram cannot evade his imprisonment in a world without objective certainties, he is able to penetrate many of the mysteries which characterize the isolated positions of its inhabitants. It is part of Tristram's weakness that he is attracted to Walter's hypotheses at the same time that he is aware of their gratuitous nature. It is also an indication of his strength. His consciousness is more inclusive and critical. For him (here he differs from Locke) wit is the superior faculty. He delights in its exercise, in the discovery of paradox, in the revelation of irony. If he frequently cannot differentiate or order, he can (and always does) enjoy the spectacle of a kaleidoscope world whose component parts are endlessly shifting and recombining to present each individual observer with a uniquely formed totality.

Tristram's hobbyhorse is the book he is writing: "What a rate have I gone on at, curvetting and frisking it away, two up and two down for four volumes together, without looking once behind, or even on one side of me, to see whom I trod upon!——I'll tread upon no one,——quoth I to myself when I mounted——I'll take a good rattling gallop; but I'll not hurt the poorest jack-ass upon the road——So off I set——up one lane——down another, through this turn-pike——over that, as if the arch-jockey of jockeys had got behind me" (IV.xx.298). To recount his story and offer his opinions is Tristram's way of communicating the nature of his experience. To present it with immediacy is to experience directly as he creates. The only formalism is the arbitrary order imposed by his mercurial wit. Attempting to translate his mode of perception and expression into the major work of his life, Tristram unknowingly reveals the central irony of his position. He would compensate for the externally imposed failures which he must suffer as a man with the self-generated success that he will achieve as an author. "Oh, *Tristram! Tristram!* . . . the credit, which will attend thee as an author, shall counterbalance the many evils which have befallen thee as a man——thou wilt feast upon the one——when thou hast lost all sense and remembrance of the other!" (IV.xxxii.337). He defeats his purpose, however, because his work is a truer reflection of his perverse vision than he is able to appreciate. In accordance with his view of the world as a half-mad system of arbitrary relationships, Tristram obligingly dons a fool's cap in which to face his audience,[5] although he does, on occasion, insist upon the real presence, the face behind the fool's grin: . . . if I should seem now and then to trifle upon the road,——or should sometimes put on a fool's cap with a bell to it, for a moment or two as we pass along,—— don't fly off,——but rather courteously give me credit for a little more wisdom than appears upon my outside . . ." (I.vi.11). He is

5. Martin Esslin, *The Theatre of the Absurd*, pp. 231–33, points out that the tradition of the clown derives from the mime plays of antiquity in which the clown's absurd behavior reflected his inability to understand simple logical relationships. The court jester who descended from the MIMUS was characterized by his inverted logic, his use of false syllogisms, free associations, and real or feigned madness.

so dominated by the cheerful, exaggerated inconsistency of his li-
centious wit that his art becomes merely another facet of his determination. The control, as we shall see, is Sterne's. The failure is
Tristram's. His curious, confusing relationship with the reader, his
exuberant enjoyment of baroque rhetoric, his love of paradox, and
his indulgence in verbal practical jokes all combine to make a seeming mockery of artistic form.

In a curious way, then, the dichotomies which plague Walter are
oddly transmuted in Tristram. Walter's delight in the functioning
of mind becomes in the more aware Tristram an enjoyment of the
possibilities of wit. Walter's adherence to rationality carries him into
an abstract world that has no parallel in reality. Tristram's creation
of paradox provides us with linguistic and intellectual patterns that
comment upon reality while trapping us in the limitations of his
subjective and eccentric awareness. As Walter's obsession with reason causes his denial of spontaneity, Tristram's love of the metaphorical defies the exertion of control and makes a great irony of
his central purpose—to know and explain. Both escape into an area
in which action and expression are deprived of their effectiveness.

Yorick.—Between Walter and Tristram stands Yorick, the third and
most firmly grounded "man of reason," who suggests still another
possibility for the functioning of the rational mind, and another
ironic example of frustration and disappointment. Since Tristram, as
the narrator, functions largely outside of the novel's action, and since
the nature of his relationship with the reader prevents him from
being completely reliable as a reporter, Yorick is useful in providing
a norm against which the other characters can be measured. When
Yorick meets the effete or unnatural, his response is pure practicality: "I wish, *Yorick*, said my father, you had read *Plato*; for there
you would have learnt that there are two LOVES——I know there
were two RELIGIONS, replied *Yorick*, amongst the ancients——one
——for the vulgar, and another for the learned; but I think ONE
LOVE might have served both of them very well" (VIII.xxxiii.587).
He meets the abstract with a similar kind of parry: "I wish there
was not a polemic divine, said *Yorick*, in the kingdom;——one ounce
of practical divinity——is worth a painted ship load of all their
reverences have imported these fifty years (V.xxviii.387). In short,
Yorick's hatred of the hypocritical, his ability to penetrate and un-
dermine affectation, his commonsense and uncompromised values,

and his clearsightedness in a world that seems always to be viewed in distorting mirrors, are all attributes which make him an effective commentator able to introduce a note of reason, although he is unable to effect any change in events or personality.

It is through his identification of both Tristram and Yorick with the figure of the jester that Sterne draws the closest parallel between them. As jesters they share a love of laughter, a sense of the absurd, a verbal dexterity and lively wit, a dislike of all that is not honest, and a recognition of individual eccentricity and social affectation. Further, both are raised to a level of tragi-comic seriousness and given universal reference by their closeness to death: Tristram's omnipresent sense of a fatal illness and, therefore, of the transitory; the association of Yorick with Hamlet's fool, who is himself a symbol of the impermanence of human values. There is an important difference here, however, for Tristram and Yorick are both types of the wise fool whose mockery masks sense. Tristram alone is victimized by his own wit.

As with all the central characters of *Tristram Shandy*, Yorick's personality is organized around a basic irony, a tension between the abstract and practical levels of behavior. Those qualities which seem most admirable make him vulnerable to the senseless malice of the community: ". . . it was his misfortune all his life long to bear the imputation of saying and doing a thousand things of which (unless my esteem blinds me) his nature was incapable. All I blame him for——or rather, all I blame and alternately like him for, was that singularity of his temper, which would never suffer him to take pains to set a story right with the world, however in his power. . . . he ever looked upon the inventor, the propagator and believer of an illiberal report alike so injurious to him,——he could not stoop to tell his story to them——and so trusted to time and truth to do it for him" (IV.xxvii.324). In his alienation from his congregation he becomes the very antithesis of the successful pastor: full of humanity and good will that cannot be communicated or implemented, the ineffectual and increasingly sceptical shepherd of a rebellious flock.

However, the bulk of responsibility lies not with Yorick himself but with the community, which can neither understand nor appreciate him. What they construe as Yorick's pride is revealed to be rare objectivity and modesty. Rather than disclose a flattering truth about himself, Yorick prefers to appear as a figure of low comedy:

"His character was,——he loved a jest in his heart——and as he saw himself in the true point of ridicule, he would say, he could not be angry with others for seeing him in a light, in which he so strongly saw himself . . ." (I.x.19). Similarly, his "wild way of talking" is revealed to be little more than good commonsense, and his chief indiscretion is an honesty that will not be compromised: "In a word, tho' he never sought, yet, at the same time, as he seldom shun'd occasions of saying what came uppermost, and without much ceremony;——he had but too many temptations in life, of scattering his wit and his humour,——his gibes and his jests about him.—— They were not lost for want of gathering" (I.xi.27).

Yorick shares Tristram's critical awareness, his perception of paradox, his psychological acumen. But he is not limited by Tristram's obsessive concern with ambiguity. His associations and his style are controlled and direct. Therefore, he cannot, like the brothers Shandy, be betrayed by the subjectivity within, by a disparity between his aspirations and his means of achieving them. It is for this reason that Yorick has no need of a hobbyhorse; his mount is real, if pathetic. Instead, he is betrayed by the subjectivity without— a victim of the relativity and fallibility of opinion and judgment. Although Yorick can meaningfully organize his own perceptions, these have no effect on the behavior of others. For the majority, appearance (variously perceived) is reality. It is Yorick's comprehension of the values that belie appearance that is the cause of his estrangement from the community which he would serve.

Toby.—Although none of the other characters is idealized in the way that Yorick is, there are others who, with Tristram, share Yorick's corrective function. For Sterne, a simple commonsense perspective is the *sine qua non* that can cut through illusion and hypocrisy. To the extent that they possess this kind of perspective, both Toby and Trim contain within themselves an antidote to their own eccentricities, a corrective of total obsession. Toby's intuitive responses ground him in the matter at hand. Because he is dominated by his emotions, which are in turn stimulated by the particular event, his attention, once fixed, is tenacious. His mind rejects the more tortuous paths of abstraction which delight the sophisticated intelligence. Thus, when he attends the visitation dinner with his brother, so that they may determine the possibility of changing Tristram's name, he and Yorick are alone in remembering their purpose. His naïve directness and modesty contrast sharply with the Scholastics' self-concerned quibbling over problems of legality, church history, and semantics. When Toby learns that the members of the court had ruled unanimously that the Duchess of Suffolk was not of kin to her own child, he asks a question that a concern for human values necessitates, a simple question that indicates with naïve curiosity the absurdity of applying abstract reasoning to fundamental human issues: "And what said the duchess of *Suffolk* to it? said my uncle *Toby*" (IV.xxix.330). It is essentially the same as his response to Walter's attempts at recounting the various reasons suggested by philosophers to explain short and long noses: "There is no cause but one . . . why one man's nose is longer than another's, but because that God pleases to have it so" (III.xli.240).

But for all of Toby's directness, he cannot keep himself from becoming involved in one of the most puzzling paradoxes of the Shandys' altogether puzzling universe. Expressed through his hobby-horsical love of military campaigns, this involvement is the most extreme sign of his inability to function in *any* but a subjective world. He is not tempted by the elaborate, abstract exercises of reason, and is not even able to use logical concepts to explain that kind of experience which does not directly impinge upon his own. For this reason he can only communicate on a limited, primarily intuitive level. The only kind of experience with which he is equipped to deal is that which refers to fundamental human emotions. Thus his wisdom is nurtured on simplicity and develops from an absolute inability to comprehend multiplicity. This differs substantially from the sophisticated, philosophical awareness that is Yorick's.

There is never any question about Toby's humanity. His possession of this quality is established early in the novel when we are allowed to hear him addressing an imprisoned fly: "I'll not hurt a hair of thy head:——Go, says he, lifting up the sash, and opening his hand as he spoke, to let it escape;——go poor devil, get thee gone, why should I hurt thee?——This world surely is wide enough to hold thee and me" (II.xii.113). The story of Le Fever provides us with indisputable proof of his benevolence, as it does of his loyalty, tenderness, optimism, and total susceptibility. Taken together they explain Hazlitt's observation that "uncle Toby is one of the finest compliments ever paid to human nature."[6] Taken together they

6. Quoted in Alan B. Howes, *Yorick and the Critics: Sterne's Reputation in England, 1760–1868*, p. 112.

also underscore the paradox of Toby's hobby: the obsession of a man of love with the forms and procedures of war. Like all of the Shandy obsessions, his contains an element of the universal. Toby himself hints at this in his odd explanation of belief that the ox is a more suitable animal than the bull to stand symbolically with woman as the founder of society: "For when the ground was tilled, said my uncle *Toby*, and made worth inclosing, then they began to secure it by walls and ditches, which was the origin of fortification" (V.xxxi. 391). Toby does recognize that war is a fundamental expression of some basic biological need: "If, when I was a school-boy, I could not hear a drum beat, but my heart beat with it——was it my fault?——Did I plant the propensity there?——did I sound the alarm within, or Nature?" (VI.xxxii.460). But his recognition is marvelously limited: marvelous in its human misunderstanding and in its self-deception, for Toby's justification of his obsession is a brilliant network of truth and falsity, of petty detail and grand concern. It is a sincere and flawed attempt to make intelligible the classically obscure relationship of ends and means. It is a testimony to the thoroughness of the paradox, the intensity of the conflict between the illusion and the reality. Questioned about the way in which man is shaped for the terrors of war, Toby responds: "——But why did you not add, *Yorick*,——if not by NATURE—— that he is so by NECESSITY?——For what is war? what is it, *Yorick*, when fought as ours has been . . . upon principles of *honour*—— what is it, but the getting together of quiet and harmless people, with their swords in their hands, to keep the ambitious and the turbulent within bounds? And heaven is my witness, brother *Shandy*, that the pleasure I have taken in these things,——and that infinite delight, in particular, which has attended my sieges in my bowling green, has arose within me, and I hope in the corporal too, from that consciousness we both had, that in carrying them on, we were answering the great ends of our creation" (VI.xxxii.462).

The most striking part of Toby's defense lies in its conclusion: in the confusion of the game with its object. Indeed, it is the extent to which Toby is unable to differentiate between the two, the extent to which one becomes a complete substitute for the other, that makes Toby's obsession so fascinating and invests it with a psychological validity of its own. Toby's explanation of his motivations and his description of the development of his interest suggest that the grim-

mest aspects of war have been repressed in much the same way that
he has escaped from an awareness of his wound. In a sense, the
affliction of his wound represents the only infusion of the ideal with
the real—in this case, a physical fact that cannot be denied.

Significantly, it is not Toby's instinct for life that restores his
health. His wound, a scar from the contact of mind and body with
the undeniable fact of war, is healed when the reality is made acceptable: when it is, in effect, sublimated. "The desire of life and
health is implanted in man's nature;——the love of liberty and
enlargement is a sister-passion to it: These my uncle *Toby* had in
common with his species;——and either of them had been sufficient
to account for his earnest desire to get well and out of doors;——
but I have told you before that nothing wrought with our family
after the common way;——and from the time and manner in which
this eager desire shew'd itself in the present case, the penetrating
reader will suspect that there was some other cause or crotchet for
it in my uncle *Toby*'s head . . ." (II.iv.92). The cause is Trim's
creation of a game that has all the fascinations of war, drawing its
inspiration, progress, and form from actual campaigns, but sharing
none of war's horrors. It is, in effect, a concretization of the meaning
which war has always had for Toby. And the soldier's fidelity to (as
well as Tristram's description of) the smallest details having to do
with the accoutrements and techniques of battle gives the illusion
its reality for both Toby and the reader. At the same time, the irony
of the exquisite complications of warfare—the rational control of
that which is a sign of man's irrationality—is underlined.

Of course, the irony is always reciprocal. If reality gives the lie
to Toby's illusion, that illusion—harmless in the protected quiet of
the bowling green—accentuates the questionable concomitants of his
noble utterances: ". . . the knowledge of arms tends so apparently
to the good and quiet of the world——and particularly that branch
of it which we have practised together in our bowling-green, has no
object but to shorten the strides of AMBITION, and intrench the lives
and the fortunes of the *few* from the plunderings of the *many* . . ."
(IX.viii.609–10). Although Toby's wholehearted, childish immersion
in his hobby has its delightful side, there is a more menacing aspect
to it in his dependence for the continuation of his play upon the
continuation of actual combat and in his sorrow at the signing of the
Peace of Utrecht.

It is further significant that when the regrettable peace forces Toby to turn from the delights of war, it is by the lures of love that he is tempted.[7]

> ——No more was he to dream, he had fixed the royal standard upon the tower of the *Bastile*, and awake with it streaming in his head.
> ——Softer visions,——gentler vibrations stole sweetly in upon his slumbers;——the trumpet of war fell out of his hands, ——he took up the lute, sweet instrument! of all others the most delicate! the most difficult!——how wilt thou touch it, my dear uncle *Toby*? (VI.xxxv.466)

That his immersion in military affairs had been a substitute for romance is suggested by this comparison of Toby, about to embark on his bowling-green adventure, with an ardent lover: "Never did lover post down to a belov'd mistress with more heat and expectation, than my uncle *Toby* did, to enjoy this self-same thing in private" (II.v.98).

Toby's new excursion into romance with the Widow Wadman serves the same purpose as his experimentation with the war games. They represent different expressions of the same impulse and, just as the complications of the game offered an escape from the harsher realities of the wound, so too with the maneuvers of love. Unfortunately for Toby, it is not as easy with the Widow Wadman to cloak the reality in the illusion. In the first place, he is not as familiar with the rules and procedures of this contest: ". . . he knew not (as my father had reproach'd him), so much as the right end of a Woman from the wrong, and therefore was never altogether at his ease near any one of them——unless in sorrow or distress; then infinite was his pity . . ." (IX.iii.602–603). In the second place, the game cannot be played for an extended period of time. The campaign is brief and the victor is expected to claim his reward. Just as Toby does not want the rewards of war—he bemoans the signing of the treaty, for it means that the reality must deny the illusion—neither does he wish to claim the reward of this other combat, sexual fulfillment. His wound, the only reality with which Toby must cope although he will never fully comprehend it, hinders him and negates the possibility of sublimation. When the crisis arrives he can only sidestep

7. A. R. Towers, "Sterne's Cock and Bull Story," also discusses the role of displacement in Toby's hobby.

the issue and withdraw. When asked his reasons for wishing to marry, he replies, "They are written . . . in the Common-Prayer Book" (IX.xxv.634). Finding himself put off by the Widow's indelicate concern, he trades the new hobby for the old pleasures and proceeds to read about the Siege of Jericho (IX.xxv.635). The frustrations, tragic as well as comic, are inherent in the paradox of his situation.

Toby and Walter.—As we have observed with regard to Walter and Tristram, the hobbyhorse can be seen as a result of the individual's method of perceiving and his mode of expression. In other words, it provides the bridge between the world of thought and the world of action. The confidence in the power of wit and reason which is shared by Tristram and his father extends also to their love of rhetoric, their fascination with forms of expression. Both interests are reflected in their "hobbyhorsical" preoccupations. Toby, on the other hand, is not a man of thought and expression. He is rather the man of feeling and action. With significant irony Sterne interrupts Toby, in his first dramatic scene, after Toby has repeated the words "I think . . . I think." He is left gesturing mutely with his pipe as Tristram begins a long digression (I.xxi.63), and is picked up later when the long pause is lamely concluded: "I think, replied he,——it would not be amiss, brother, if we rung the bell" (II.vi.99).

Toby's early love of the military reflects his adherence to simple, formularized values as well as his desire to express himself directly through action. Sustaining his wound, he is not only forced into contact with a harsh, irrefutable reality, but is also, in his attempt to describe clearly the place and circumstances of his mishap, forced to rely upon language and abstract reasoning: ". . . the many perplexities he was in, arose out of the almost insurmountable difficulties he found in telling his story intelligibly, and giving such clear ideas of the differences and distinctions between the scarp and the counterscarp,——the glacis and covered way,——the half-moon and ravelin,——as to make his company fully comprehend where and what he was about" (II.i.82). In a sense, it is his inability to master language that is responsible for the perpetuation of his sickness. As Tristram explains: "T'was not by ideas,——by heaven! his life was put in jeopardy by words" (II.ii.87). His hobby is born from his lack of verbal success, and with his new-found approximation of action comes also an approximation of health. Still, when he attempts to function anywhere beyond this play world of soldiers and campaigns, when he attempts to communicate with anyone whose interests and responses differ to any extent from his own, he faces the same acute problems. Because of the polar differences that exist in Toby's and Walter's perceptions of the world, their relationship emphasizes the propensities and weaknesses of each.

It is necessary to recognize the depth of feeling, the good will and common sympathy, that exists between the two brothers. Typical is Toby's immediate response to Trim's explanation of the Widow Wadman's repeated inquiries into the nature of his wound: "————Let us go to my brother *Shandy's*, said he" (IX.xxxi.643). Nor is Walter's attachment to Toby any less strong. "He was, however, frank and generous in his nature;——at all times open to conviction; and in the little ebullitions of this subacid humour toward others, but particularly toward my uncle *Toby*, whom he truly loved;——he would feel more pain, ten times told (except in the affair of my aunt *Dinah*, or where an hypothesis was concerned) than what he ever gave" (II.xii.114). But Toby is as little able to overcome the pressure of Walter's rhetoric to discover his meaning as he is able to overcome the narrowness of his own associations. And the nature of Toby's customary response is a constant cause of disturbance to Walter: ". . . it is one of the most unaccountable problems that ever I met with in my observations of human nature, that nothing should prove my father's mettle so much, or make his passions go off so like gun-powder, as the unexpected strokes his science met with from the quaint simplicity of my uncle *Toby's* questions" (III. xli.239). Even when Walter vows that he will never again tease his brother about his hobbyhorse, his own language—reflecting the irresistible attraction that the subject has for him—undercuts the force of his intention. "May my brains be knock'd out with a battering ram or a catapulta, I care not which, quoth my father to himself, ——if ever I insult this worthy soul more" (III.xxiv.212). When the brothers do respond to one another's pronouncements, the cause can always be traced to a misinterpretation growing out of a private association. Thus Walter, at one point, becomes interested in Toby's discussion of fortification because he finds in it ripe ground for a dissertation upon trade (II.xiv.117–18). Or Toby wrongly defines a word when there is more than one possible meaning that could be assigned to it. " 'Tis a pity, said my father, that truth can only be on one side, brother *Toby*,——considering what ingenuity these learned men have all shewn in their solutions of noses.——Can noses be dissolved? replied my uncle *Toby*" (III.xli.239). But more often than not Toby merely provides Walter with a convenient presence at which he can philosophize. Unhappily Walter is doomed to be a teacher who cannot teach since Toby is the student incapable of learning.

The irony of their relative positions is continually emphasized by the effect which each unconsciously achieves, an effect that seems frequently to stand in direct contradiction to the one intended or expected. It is with good reason that uncle Toby is compared to the Cynic philosopher Diogenes, who refuted the arguments of Zeno against motion: ". . . the Philosopher would use no other argument to the sceptic, who disputed with him against the reality of motion, save that of rising up upon his legs, and walking a-cross the room . . ." (I.xxiv.78). For the irrefutable simplicity of Toby's commonsense response seems often to contain more relevance, more meaning, more profound intuition, than all of Walter's elaborate theorizing.

> As the antients agree, brother *Toby*, said my father, that there are two different and distinct kinds of *love*, according to the different parts which are affected by it——the Brain or Liver ——I think when a man is in love, it behoves him a little to consider which of the two he is fallen into.
>
> What signifies it, brother *Shandy*, replied my uncle *Toby*, which of the two it is, provided it will but make a man marry, and love his wife, and get a few children. (VIII.xxxiii.585–86)

Of course, there is another, deeper irony here that is inherent in the nature of their lives. Walter, despite his analytical and rational approach, has married and begotten children, while Toby, although not lacking in feelings proper to his sex, seems doomed to a childless bachelorhood. It is but another example of the illusory and deceptive effect of language in its tenuous relation to thought and its more tenuous relation to reality.

Similarly, Toby's gestures, his facial expressions, his habit of whistling Lillabullero "when anything shocked or surprised him;—— but especially when any thing, which he deem'd very absurd, was offered" (I.xxi.69), all declare the impotence of language, its inferiority to a more delicate and subtle method of communication. Meaning shines through the intuitive response while it is hidden beneath the obliquity of the complex, carefully planned utterance.

Trim.—Trim and Toby's relationship offers the only example of communication on an explicitly verbal as well as a mute, intuitive level. The irony of their relationship consists of the domination of master by servant, for although Toby frequently acts as a kindly guardian to Trim, gently reprimanding his lapses of taste, it is Trim who draws the pattern for their lives and emerges as the stronger, more lucid of the two. Trim is more consistent than any of the Shandys. He is not ruled so much by an obsession as he is by a kindly understanding of his master's needs and a sincere concern for the practice of basic moral and humanitarian precepts.

Although it is true that Trim is willing to mount Toby's hobby-horse and share with him a total imaginative immersion in the minutiae of their play battles, one does not feel that he is as deeply committed. He delights in his own inventiveness in working out the details of their game, and he is not immune to the delights of play, but his real interest is in his master's well-being. His purpose is therapeutic; when one form of therapy becomes impractical, he throws himself without regret into the development of the next possibility, the romance with the Widow Wadman.

If Trim could be said to have a hobbyhorse of his own, it would be this: "The fellow lov'd to advise,——or rather to hear himself talk . . ." (II.v.95). Trim is an orator, and because he is a subtle mixture of the intuitively artful and the intuitively artless, he functions as a foil for both Toby and Walter. A central irony of his characterization grows out of the paradox developed between art and nature.[8] Trim is the natural orator whose instinct approximates art. Nevertheless, he is unable to differentiate art from nature and can only comprehend fiction when it is reduced to concrete terms. He resorts, as does Toby, to the use of gesture and posture in order to express himself; but while Toby's dependence is clearly the result of impotence before language, Trim's bears the force of intention. Asked for an opinion, he formally arranges himself in a particular attitude before replying: "Prithee *Trim*, said *Yorick*, without staying

8. See William S. Farrell, "Nature vs. Art as a Comic Pattern in *Tristram Shandy*." Farrell discusses at length the expression of the art-nature paradox in the rhetorical patterns of the novel.

for my father's leave,——tell us honestly——what is thy opinion concerning this self same radical heat and radical moisture? . . . The corporal put his hat under his left arm, and with his stick hanging upon the wrist of it, by a black thong split into a tassel about the knot, he marched up to the ground where he had performed his catechism; then touching his under jaw with the thumb and fingers of his right hand before he opened his mouth,——he delivered his notion thus" (V.xxxviii.400). But his knowledge of the gesture which can most effectively be employed, the posture which can most eloquently be assumed, is intuitive. It is prompted by his fine sense of the dramatic and facilitated by a matter-of-fact acceptance of his own body.

Trim's rhetoric—indeed his whole method of approaching and interpreting the objective world—is characterized by his common-sense perspective, literalness, and lack of imagination. Unlike Walter, he is never led astray by a richly fabricating wit or a playful fancy. Trim tends always to particularize the abstract and translates everything into experiential terms. He is unable to differentiate between imaginative materials and phenomenological occurrences, although he is himself, in his instinct for rhetoric, presented as an artist. He must submerge the work of art and the theoretical formulation in the chaotic mass of personal experience. His emotional rendering of Yorick's sermon "On Conscience" demonstrates this, just as the responses of Toby, Walter, and Dr. Slop to his reading comprise a statement about their epistemological and aesthetic orientations.

In Walter's and Trim's responses to Bobby's death we are given "two orators . . . contrasted by nature and education, haranguing over the same bier" (V.vi.359). Walter's route, which proceeds by way of metaphor, reference, and allusion, is a circuitous one, while Trim, we are told, goes "strait forwards as nature could lead him, to the heart" (V.vi.359). His speech is the more effective of the two, for it is not obscured by the oddments of learning. Trim is, in a sense, the ideal orator, for his rhetoric is an expression of the whole man. His eloquence is derived from his conviction of the correctness of his cause and reflects the generosity of his heart and the strength of his values. In this sense he satisfies the classical Platonic rules of oratory. While Walter's primary concerns are intellectual and aesthetic (this is true of his perceptions as well as his mode of expression), Trim's orientation is principally moral. He deals in clear absolutes, never recognizing that more than one meaning may be assigned to a value term. Thus, when Dr. Slop gives his permission for Trim to read the sermon on the grounds that they all take equal risks on which side of the church it is written, Trim replies: " 'Tis wrote upon neither side . . . for 'tis only upon *Conscience*, an' please your Honours," (II.xvi.120). Trim's naïve simplicity does more here to undercut the doctor's position than would a direct attack. He produces a similar effect with similar means when he speaks of the misfortunes of people he has known, while Walter lies prostrated after learning that Tristram's nose has been crushed in the birth process:

> O!——these are misfortunes, cried *Trim*,——pulling out his handkerchief——these are misfortunes, may it please your honour, worth lying down and crying over.
> ——My father could not help blushing. (IV.iv.275)

Trim emerges as a more balanced human being than most of Sterne's other characters. Through his morality and humanity, the world of thought and the world of action are united, and there is no disparity created between his aspiration and the reality against which it is measured. His judgments are not marred by Walter's eccentricities or Toby's unknowing optimism, and both perspective and deliberation mark his actions. That the functioning of his body is as normal as the functioning of his mind and conscience—typified by the same easy acceptance and righteous confidence—is made clear by his relationship with Bridget. Walter, Toby, and Tristram are unable, for a combination of physical and psychological reasons, to allow themselves the satisfactions of normal sexual pleasures. Walter and Toby find their escapes in games of the intellect and the imagination. Tristram finds his in art and in a harmless but frustrated sentimentality.

Thus, on one side we have Toby's unnatural modesty and the Widow Wadman's elaborate machinations as she attempts to discover the extent and significance of Toby's wound. In contrast, we are given Trim's and Bridget's direct acceptance of the real issue. What is illegitimate curiosity in the widow becomes justifiable concern in the maid. The cause, one infers, lies in the readiness of the suitors and the attitudes of the social groups to which they belong: ". . . and in this cursed trench, Mrs. *Bridget*, quoth the Corporal, taking her by the hand, did he receive the wound which crush'd him so miserably *here*——In pronouncing which he slightly press'd the back of her hand towards the part he felt for—and let it fall" (IX. xxviii.639). Throughout *Tristram Shandy*, Sterne demonstrates that sexual potency, as an alternative mode of communication, is a function of the whole man, reflecting his capacities and the balance of his faculties. Trim is the most normal of the people who inhabit Tristram's world. The directness of his approach and his firm grounding in the practical and realistic demand the sacrifice of his imagination but allow him to move with physical and intellectual freedom, unhampered by the irrational demands of obsession or the stringent controls of society.

Mrs. Shandy.—At the opposite end of the spectrum stands Mrs. Shandy, who is defined almost exclusively in negative terms: she is Locke's "white paper," unmarred by experience, passive in her perception of the world, seemingly unable to interpret meaningfully or express her impressions, performing her female functions more by accident than through intent. Totally lacking in imagination, she is also without curiosity: "——That she is not a woman of science, my father would say——is her misfortune——but she might ask a question" (VI.xxxix.472). A woman who prefers to remain at home knitting a pair of worsted breeches for her husband rather than joining her family on their Grand Tour, Mrs. Shandy is without ideas or interests and is therefore possessed of few associations, depending upon habit and tradition for her responses. Because her ability to learn is so restricted, she is virtually unable to express herself: "Now she had a way . . . and that was never to refuse her assent and consent to any proposition my father laid before her, merely because she did not understand it, or had no ideas to the principal word or term of art, upon which the tenet or proposition rolled. She contented herself with doing all that her godfathers and godmothers promised for her—but no more; and so would go on using a hard word twenty years together——and replying to it too, if it was a verb, in all its moods and tenses, without giving herself any trouble to enquire about it" (IX.xi.613).

There are no scenes of greater comic frustration in *Tristram Shandy* than those which present the dialogues between Tristram's mother and father: ". . . a discourse seldom went on much further betwixt them, than a proposition,——a reply, and a rejoinder; at the end of which, it generally took breath for a few minutes, (as in the affair of the breeches) and then went on again" (VI.xxxix.472). The patterns of their conversations also contain an elementary paradox. Typically, in the "Bed of Justice" which is held to decide the advisability of putting Tristram into breeches (VI.xviii.437), Mrs. Shandy's continual agreement—intellectual as well as sexual—implies criticism through its passivity. Her extreme flexibility implies a basic, mindless inflexibility and her willingness is tantamount to refusal. In her neutrality, extremes meet and negate one another. Further, their lack of communication extends to sexual matters, and their physical and intellectual incompatibility are reciprocal metaphors. Although they approach their conjugal bed from opposite extremes of temperament and orientation, Walter's accusation of his wife might with justice be applied to him as well: "You never will distinguish, Mrs. *Shandy*, nor shall I ever teach you to do it, betwixt a point of pleasure and a point of convenience.——This was on the *Sunday* night;——and further this chapter sayeth not" (VI.xviii. 438–39). The relationship between Mr. and Mrs. Shandy is one of the novel's numerous instances of the difficulties that arise when one attempts to distinguish cause from effect. Their misfortune arises not so much from their own individual circumstances as from the impossibility of combining their two temperaments. Tristram makes it clear that they share—albeit unconsciously—the responsibility for the misfortune of his destiny. "A temperate current of blood ran orderly through her veins in all months of the year, and in all critical moments both of the day and night alike. . . . And as for my father's example! 'twas so far from being either aiding or abetting thereunto, that 'twas the whole business of his life to keep all fancies of that kind out of her head . . . And here am I sitting, this 12th day of *August*, 1766, in a purple jerkin and yellow pair of slippers, without either wig or cap on, a most tragicomical completion of his prediction, "That I should neither think, nor act like any other man's child, upon that very account" (IX.i.600).

Occupying this negative position in terms of potentiality, achievement and aspiration, Mrs. Shandy plays a minor but curiously contemporary and parodic role. Northrop Frye has written in his *Anatomy of Criticism*: "To the extent that the encyclopaedic form concerns itself with the cycle of human life, an ambivalent female archetype appears in it, sometimes benevolent, sometimes sinister, but usually presiding over and confirming the cyclical movement" (p. 322). Indeed, there is in Mrs. Shandy's presence something of the universal principle of female endurance which persists amid the paradoxes of her position and her personality. She is the woman—the life-force—who remains remote and uninvolved. She is the mother who, in the earliest moments of procreation, flaws the very life she creates because she rejects her own sexuality. She is an absurd Penelope, a silent and frigid Molly Bloom. But within the peculiar, alien demands of her milieu, despite the extraordinary limitations which are imposed upon her from within and without, she does continue to function, and follows, however unenthusiastically, the patterns set down for her.

Sterne seems anxious to convey in his characterization of Mrs. Shandy a sense of an irreducible human quality—purged of all that is meaningful save an inarticulate demand for sympathy: sympathy for her personal situation and for the chaotic collection of circumstances that have created it. It seems important that we are not allowed to see her response to the news of Bobby's death. A strong response would make of her a completely different, more conventional character, and her usual passivity would in this case become intolerable. It is only by maintaining her in neutrality that Sterne can create the polar image that is more limited in its universality but not essentially different from that of all the Shandys.

Sterne follows the same basic technique with his other characters, immersing them in just enough complexity to give them depth while keeping his world sufficiently abstract. In a curious way, the qualities of characterization that are responsible for his realism are responsible also for the abstract universality. These qualities grow out of his awareness of the empiricist paradox and his desire to communicate it in specifically human terms. As we have seen, the hobbyhorse, which expresses the uniqueness of the individual, develops from the control of the external world by the internal economy peculiar to each man. The relation of rational, imaginative, and physical powers determines whether the individual will function principally in a world of intellect, art, action, or instinct; this in turn determines which of the faculties and functions will remain undeveloped and even unused. In such a world, where uniqueness is confirmed by a lack of successful communication, eccentricity must be the rule.

By concentrating upon these basic functions Sterne does, of course, achieve a certain universality in his characterizations, and by keeping outside of the complexities and superficialities of a world that is defined by social values, he cannot avoid a measure of abstraction.

Because of the intensely personal nature of each man's response, all gestures toward creating a meaningful, communicable concept are made invalid—all but the attempt itself: the repeated movement outside oneself, the continuation in the face of all frustration and negation.

In some fundamental way, then, Sterne defines his characters as he organizes his structure: through diversity and eccentricity. And his people—much as the form of his book—are subject to the whims and pressures of external forces. Just as they cannot control the world outside of themselves, so too are they unable to determine the course and manner of their own lives. The irony of them all, as we have seen, is the disparity between their aspirations and the reality, their distortions of the world and their delusions about themselves. They are important because they tell us about the nature of the human mind, the nature of the human predicament, the possibility of human salvation. Together their lives compose a pattern which represents universal—not individual—potentiality and limitation. The unity of *Tristram Shandy* is thematic. Just as the form and structure work to create an image of confusion, so do the characters achieve their definition in isolation and alienation. There are dramatic scenes (vignettes) and the drama of monologue, but there is no progressive dramatic movement. The characters are part of a universal paradox, subject to the ironies that besiege their lives, motivating and defeating them. These ironies are inevitable in a completely subjective world in which neither circumstance nor language can claim absolute reference. As we shall see, it is the pattern of perversity growing out of Sterne's handling of his major themes that provides both characters and structure with a unifying context.

The Development of Themes

Fundamental to the development of all the major themes in *Tristram Shandy* is Sterne's concept of the basic modes of perception. Proceeding with the misleading appearance of randomness, Sterne systematically analyzes and reveals the weaknesses of three fundamental postures: rationality, imagination, and emotion. Although on the surface all are treated with acceptance, Sterne's irony actually undercuts each possibility, in keeping with the tentative relativity of his extreme, empirical position.

In his presentation of Walter's fantasy world and in his exposure of the follies of professional system-builders, Sterne suggests what happens when the mind becomes absorbed in its own forms. Reason is unable to deal with heterogeneity. Its propensity is for simplification and, therefore, distortion. Thus, while Walter occupies the position of "supreme rationalist," he is not objective in his adoption of any opinion: "He pick'd up an opinion, Sir, as a man in a state of nature picks up an apple.——It becomes his own,——and if he is a man of spirit, he would lose his life rather than give it up——" (III.xxiv.221). The basic trouble with the functioning of reason seems to lie with the hypothesis—the cornerstone of all theory, but the child of eccentricity and subjectivity: "It is the nature of an hypothesis, when once a man has conceived it, that it assimilates every thing to itself as proper nourishment; and, from the first moment of your begetting it, it generally grows the stronger by every thing you see, hear, read, or understand" (II.xix.151). Here Sterne suggests the psychological roots of association, the peculiarly individual and emotional nature of learning, the place of "set" in perception, the irrational sources of rationality. Nor does he restrict his analysis of the use and misuse of reason to Walter's case. The satirical disrobings of doctors, lawyers, churchmen, and academicians which run through the book are all made to serve the same end. Sterne thinks it inevitable that man, in his role of philosopher, should attempt to penetrate the mysteries of life with his rational powers: "When great or unexpected events fall out upon the stage of this sublunary world—the mind of man, which is an inquisitive kind of a substance, naturally takes a flight, behind the scenes, to see what is the cause and first spring of them . . ." (IV.xxvii.323). And he finds that the search for truth ends, most frequently and ironically, in an erroneous conclusion, as when Yorick is held responsible for Phutatorius' encounter with the hot chestnut. That which should be objectively deduced is the result of half-knowledge and personal inclination.

Sterne does not judge the role of the imagination in the processes of learning and communication more positively than he does the role of reason. Tristram joins the centuries-old debate concerning the relationship and relative merits of wit and judgment (III.xx.192–203). Defending the view that the one cannot be found without the other, Tristram's statement, filled with images, metaphors, and rambling associations, does itself stand as a delightful example of the disorderly and illogical creations produced by a lively imagination undisciplined by the laws of reason. Although Tristram opposes Locke on this issue (ironically, it is the only time that he makes his opposition explicit), Sterne seems to side more with the philosopher, and would apparently maintain with Yorick "that brisk trotting and slow argumentation, like wit and judgement, were two incompatible movements" (I.x.20). All of the central characters in *Tristram Shandy* seem to prove the impossibility of possessing these two faculties in equal measure. Tristram's novel is a testimony to his difficulties in separating the demands of art from the exigencies of life and organizing spontaneous psychic impressions and flights of fancy into a rational order that molds life and does not merely reflect it. In Trim and Toby we have the men of action who cannot escape into illusion. Toby, once he has accepted the one great leap that his game involves, neither creates new material nor escapes the limitations of reality. His hobby follows exactly the actual events of the war, and when the Peace of Utrecht has been signed there is no possibility of his contriving further action. The practicality and commonsense of Toby and Trim make them painfully literal-minded. They cannot differentiate art from life because the precision of their viewpoints and their ability to empathize make art *into* life. Toby cannot allow Trim to tell "The Story of the King of Bohemia and his Seven Castles" without clarifying matters of geography, chronology, and military procedure (VIII.xix.560–69). Trim cannot read Yorick's sermon with its references to the Inquisition without weeping for the fate of his brother Tom. In short, both misunderstand because they cannot help taking figurative language literally.

Walter, on the other hand, takes a firm stand against the excesses of the imagination, but he cannot himself resist the temptation of metaphorical language—much to the discomfort of his brother: "When I reflect, brother *Toby*, upon MAN; and take a view of that dark side of him which represents his life as open to so many causes of trouble——when I consider, brother *Toby*, how oft we eat the bread of affliction, and that we are born to it, as to the portion of our inheritance————I was born to nothing, quoth my uncle *Toby*, interrupting my father——but my commission" (IV.vii.277). Similarly, Walter meets the news of his elder son's death with an oration that is little more than a network of remembered fragments concerned with death and mortality and bears little relationship to the immediate situation (V.iii.355). His love of eccentric bits of information, his preoccupation with the creative functioning rather than with the objects of mind, and his aspiration to eloquence all tend to carry him away from reality into a fanciful world which is impervious to the distinctions of judgment.

Sterne, then, emphasizes the tendencies of the reason and the imagination to behave autonomously, sealing the agent in a vacuum of subjectivity that makes his isolation inevitable. As critical faculties of perception and interpretation they are found wanting, dependent upon environmental and psychological factors, erroneously claiming a measure of universality.

There is still another possible posture and literary style which is related to emotional apprehension. Offered as a mode of cognition to be set beside reason and imagination, "emotionality" is the inarticulate condition of Toby and Walter's relationship. It frequently provides the basis for the commonsense perceptions of Yorick and Trim, and, in its early, reflexive stage, is the underlying motive for most of the choices and decisions that claim reason as their progenitor. In *Tristram Shandy* it is emotional predilection that determines, for example, the birth and development of Walter's systems as well as the structuring of Tristram's aesthetic materials. In *A Sentimental Journey* it is emotional predisposition that affords Yorick his psychological and social insights rather than abstractions of logic. In its fundamental state it is an irrational and divisive principle: a function of pure subjectivity, the *sine qua non* of behavior, responsible for both the choice of expressive forms and their failure in communication. In sentimentality (the advanced stage of development) there is a desire to socialize and channel natural emotionalism. The question of its place in Sterne's work has been the cause of more interest and more misunderstanding than any other aspect of the novel. In his own time his sentimentality aroused the greatest admiration. In our time it is treated with suspicion. Both attitudes have rested largely upon an erroneous belief in his undeviating seriousness.

In his exploration of emotional response, Sterne was doing more than indulging a personal weakness. He was actually sharing in a vital philosophical and psychological concern of his age. Originating

with the Latitudinarian churchmen as a reaction against the mate-
rialism of Thomas Hobbes, the philosophy postulated the natural
goodness of man and urged the rehabilitation of passions by advo-
cating the positive virtues of cheerfulness, charity, and benevolence.[1]
Locke added the strength of a systematic approach to this position.
He emphasized the role of sensation and insisted upon the relation
of man's natural goodness and sociability to his adherence to a
pleasure-pain principle. Locke's view was supported by Shaftesbury's
optimistic belief in instinctual benevolence expressed through a phi-
lanthropy that was its own reward. The theory was developed with
greatest sophistication by Hume, who claimed that "the minds of all
men are similar in their feelings and operations, nor can any one be
actuated by any affection, of which all others are not, in some degree,
susceptible. As in strings equally wound up, the motion of one communicates itself to the rest; so all the affections readily pass from
one person to another, and beget correspondent movements in every
human creature. When I see the effects of passion in the voice and
gesture of any person, my mind immediately passes from these
effects to their causes, and forms such a lively idea of the passion,
as is presently converted into the passion itself. In like manner,
when I perceive the *causes* of any emotion, my mind is convey'd
to the effects, and is actuated with a like emotion."[2] Sterne shares
Hume's belief in the possibility of a man's "entering into the senti-
ments of others." This concept does in fact become the cornerstone
of his ethical and social philosophy, and he explores its psychological implications as well as its relation to other, frequently ambivalent functions of personality.

Sentimentality, according to Sterne's view, is a self-conscious stage
in the development of the empathic process. It is a self-induced state
of empathy which attempts to retain the valuable elements of instinctual emotionality. The actual relation of the self-conscious to
the instinctual is difficult to determine. Because natural emotion is
easily undermined by the self-conscious and stylized response, Sterne
credits most readily the dignity and validity of intuitional feelings
which are simply expressed. Thus Toby, who is without the guile
of the wit or the intellect, comes the closest to being a man of true

---

1. Gardner D. Stout, Jr., studies *Sentimental Journey* from this perspective
in his essay, "Yorick's *Sentimental Journey:* A Comic Pilgrim's Progress for
the Man of Feeling."

2. *A Treatise of Human Nature*, pp. 575–76.

sentiment, while Tristram and the journeying Yorick, whose minds and imaginations set wider boundaries for their aspirations, frequently lapse into bathetic and ludicrous postures.

In *Tristram Shandy*, sentimentality is presented as one of many psychological responses and a predominantly nonverbal mode of communication. As the subject of *A Sentimental Journey*, its implications are more subtly explored. Rufus Putney suggests, quite rightly, that Sterne became interested in the pathetic as his audience demonstrated its enthusiasm for Uncle Toby and the story of Le Fever.[3] But this interest did, in fact, represent more than a simple nod to popular taste. It was a function of Sterne's need to discover a means of escape from the epistemological cul-de-sac in which he had found himself. In *Tristram Shandy*, Sterne had offered empathy as the only viable alternative to the frustrated failures of communication. Despite the fact that its practitioners were largely mute and its practical results impossible to measure, empathy remained a beacon of possibility, shining unmistakably—if dimly—in the dense fog of isolation. In *A Sentimental Journey*, Sterne explored, through Yorick, the true value of the light: its ability to cheer the wearisome voyage and unite the conscious and unconscious selves of the troubled voyager. Tristram's grand tour is a flight from death and a journey into life: a journey of the imagination as it seems to create personal meaning in the face of impersonal absurdity. Yorick's journey represents the lifelong quest of the emotional being for a practical definition of the relation of psychological need and ethical value. Yorick, more rational and self-analytical than Toby, is more likely than he to discover the potentialities as well as the ironic limitations of the sentimental mode: the rewards and dangers that await the sentimental traveler.

The rewards are similar to those experienced by Toby and, at times, by Tristram. They are all intuitive and sensory in nature: the fleeting, satisfying moment of communication through gesture and expression; the feeling of physical and spiritual well-being which is the result of benevolent action; the increased capacity for pleasure and enjoyment which accompanies willing receptivity. The dangers are more complex and belong to varied levels of experience. There are, for example, the comic incongruities which result from the confrontation of illusion by reality. There is the squeaking door hinge

---

3. "The Evolution of *A Sentimental Journey*."

which belies the ineffectuality of Walter's theory; the insensitive postilion who gallops along unconcernedly, destroying Yorick's melancholy moment of mourning,[4] and the Grisset's husband, who takes Yorick by surprise as he feels, so tenderly, the lady's pulse.

And there are also the more subtle difficulties which grow from the ambiguous nature of sentimentality itself, relating it to Sterne's psychological and philosophical subjectivism. In *Tristram Shandy*, Sterne demonstrates the relativity of all knowledge and perception. In *A Sentimental Journey*, he suggests the potentially solipsistic nature of all empathic experience. He reveals how difficult it is to be certain of the objective validity of the emotion one projects onto another, for the act of projection is imaginative, fundamentally subjective, and therefore belongs to the more inclusive process of self-investigation. The sympathetic identification of oneself with another is an act of interpretation. Like all acts of interpretation, like Tristram's novel, it is possessed in some way of creative force, of aesthetic value, and it refers ultimately back to its source: the self. From this point of view empathy is a complex game of role-playing. The subject, in the process of social interaction, experiences not the feelings of the "other" but the responses of himself: himself as vain, benevolent, affectionate, petty. Thus, Tristram approaches Maria, hoping to pierce and share the mystery of her madness. He is presented, instead, with a puzzle of his own nature:

> MARIA look'd wistfully for some time at me, and then at her goat——and then at me——and then at her goat again, and so on alternately——
> Well, *Maria*, said I softly——what resemblance do you find? (IX.xxiv.631)

Hearing Tristram's account of this meeting, Yorick is so affected by it (he tells us in *A Sentimental Journey*) that he decides to go half a league out of his way in order to avail himself of a similar opportunity. He is not disappointed. He finds that he too can empathize with the distraught girl. But the explicit recognition which he finally makes is no more relevant to Maria's own condition than was Tristram's. It is a recognition—slightly self-congratulatory—of the extent to which he is himself capable of feeling:

4. Laurence Sterne, *A Sentimental Journey Through France and Italy*, ed. Gardner D. Stout, Jr. (Berkeley, 1967), pp. 142–44. All succeeding references are to this edition and will be given within the text.

> I sat down close by her; and Maria let me wipe (the tears) away as they fell with my handkerchief.———I then steep'd it in my own——and then in hers——and then in mine——and then I wip'd hers again——and as I did it, I felt such undescribable emotions within me as I am sure could not be accounted for from any combinations of matter and motion.
>
> I am positive I have a soul; nor can all the books with which materialists have pester'd the world ever convince me of the contrary. (*Sentimental Journey*, p. 271).

The man of feeling stands at the center of experience, replacing the man of reason. *Sentio ergo sum* is his motto. His sensations are proof of his existence—important, therefore, for their own sake, easily viewed as ends in themselves.

It is appropriate that Yorick should carry the starling's image as the crest in his arms.[5] The plight of the caged bird is a rich metaphor for the condition of the man shut up in the prison of his own subjectivity, and it extends to include specific aspects of both their situations. Yorick, for example, finds that it is impossible to free the starling from its cruel confinement: "God help thee! said I, but I'll let thee out, cost what it will; so I turn'd about the cage to get to the door; it was twisted and double twisted so fast with wire, there was no getting it open without pulling the cage to pieces . . ." (*Sentimental Journey*, p. 197).

It is impossible, in a similar way, for Yorick to free his own soul from the confinement of his body and the limitations of his subjective being, "without pulling the cage to pieces." Then, too, the starling's pilgrimage from Lord A to Lord B to Lord C, "half round the alphabet" and into the lower house, proves to be an exercise in futility. To all he repeats the plaintive statement of his pathetic situation, "I can't get out——I can't get out," but he meets with little response. Each being is defined and set apart by his own self-inflicted brand of imprisonment: ". . . as all these wanted to get in ——and my bird wanted to get out——he had almost as little store set by him in London as in Paris" (*Sentimental Journey*, p. 205). Yorick is similarly defeated in his attempt to unite the island with the mainland: England with the continent, himself with society. His

---

5. The starling was used as the emblematic crest of the Sterne family. Stout points out the clear association between "starling"—dialectical *starn* (fr. OE *stearn*), Latin *sturnus*, and Sterne, p. 206.

journey, which carries him from the monk to the beggars, to the grisset, to the fille de chambre, is ultimately as frustrating as the starling's quest for a permanent home.

Yorick tells us that he is a man "interested in his own sensations" (22). The twentieth-century reader is struck by the extent to which this eighteenth-century sentimentalist is the victim of a modern malaise: self-consciousness. Always taking his own emotional temperature, Yorick recognizes all too well the selfish vanity which tortures the most benevolent action: "We get forwards in the world not so much by doing services, as receiving them: you take a withering twig, and put it in the ground; and then you water it, because you have planted it" (*Sentimental Journey*, p. 261). Always searching out the motive and analyzing his response, Yorick translates the role of the jester into peculiarly contemporary terms. Isolation is revealed to be part of the human condition. The jester is no longer seen as social critic. He is the wise philosopher whose only reference is himself. He is the victim of his own irony: insightful and confused. Self-consciousness brings knowledge, but it distorts perspective. This jester cannot be as effective as his ancestors because, unlike them, he is unable to "get out." They could stand back from the society in order to comment and direct. He cannot escape the limitations of his identity.

In Yorick's journey the implications of Tristram's experience are made clear. Emotion deeply felt can easily lapse into bathos:

> ———Tender and faithful spirits! cried I, addressing myself to *Amandus* and *Amanda*———long———long have I tarried to drop this tear upon your tomb———I come———I come
>
> ———
>
> When I came———there was no tomb to drop it upon.
> What would I have given for my uncle *Toby* to have whistled, Lillo bullero! (VII.xl.532)

When valid, as Yorick knows, the developed sensibility provides a link with the "great sensorium of the world" (*Sentimental Journey*, p. 278), but as soon as it is valued for its own sake, as Yorick demonstrates, it verges on prurience or morbidity: the tragi-comic expression of the clown transformed into the lecherous leer or the self-pitying whimper. Inarticulate emotion seems deepest, but its quality remains essentially unknown. Once articulated, it is easily exaggerated and debased. Even when it is well-articulated, as in

Tristram's poetic speech about time ("Time wastes too fast: every letter I trace tells me with what rapidity Life follows my pen . . ." [IX.viii.610–11]), there is the embarrassed pause that follows the outburst, and then the ironic self-parody ("Now for what the world thinks of that ejaculation——I would not give a groat . . ." [IX.ix. 611]). The expression of feeling does not create a bridge between people. It rather emphasizes their distance and separation.

So the image of Locke appears again. Another paradox is presented: Toby the military man who finds the world large enough to hold both himself *and* a fly; Tristram, who sympathetically offers an ass one of his macaroons, only to realize that "there was more of pleasantry in the conceit of seeing *how* an ass would eat a macaroon ——than of benevolence in giving him one" (VI.xxxii.524); Yorick watering—very likely with his tears—the withering twig which he has planted *because* he has planted it. The contradictions are there; but the philosophical irony is complex and makes of each part of the contradiction a truth. In the Shandean world, which is our own, we learn once again that man's only consistency is that he is inconsistent. The book that Yorick writes marks his attempt (it parallels Tristram's) to turn his journey into a quest: a quest for the self in the morality of sensibility. Because Sterne's philosophical position marks Yorick as another anti-hero, the quest can have no end. Its end, like the fille de chambre's END, is just another beginning.

Language.—The form of *Tristram Shandy* is also its subject. As Tristram's attempt to share his vision with the reader, the novel's form is related to the general problem of communication. The ironic pattern which marks the progress of this relationship of form and subject is echoed in other, similar attempts and in other relationships. Considered together, these attempts represent Sterne's pessimistic view of the possibility of meaningful verbal expression.

Sterne gives us Walter, Tristram, and Trim, who have in common an unwavering confidence in the power of the word. In Walter's case this corresponds to a faith in the power of reason. For Tristram it is commensurate with a belief in the transforming power of wit. With Trim it seems to be the result of a simple fascination with language and a love of play-acting. All are dedicated to the art of expression. All expect to find in language a way of illuminating the mysteries of their own world and the worlds of one another. All are carried deeper and deeper into the subjective darkness that resists communication. Expression becomes for them a private exercise, practiced for their own enjoyment. Most attempts are revealed to be curiously self-defeating. Without sympathy they become futile.

In his critical consideration of language as the primary tool used (effectively or not) in the acquisition and preservation of knowledge, Sterne was, as we have seen, much influenced by Locke, who identified and analyzed the six most common abuses of language. These six categories might well have served as models for Sterne in his comedy of pretension and ignorance, for they represent the basic patterns of "learned" conversation. It is interesting to note the way in which Sterne utilizes these categories, making them flexible enough to include the eccentricities of his major characters, as well as the more generalized qualities of mind which are the targets of his satiric digressions on learning.

The first and "most palpable" abuse Locke points to is "the using of words without clear and distinct ideas." He explains that some of the words in this grouping were first introduced by philosophical and religious sects and did not have clear ideas affixed to them, while others lost their distinct meaning through usage (II.III.x.2;122–23). Sterne reveals that all three of the Shandy males are guilty on this score. Toby, with his eccentric echoing of patriotic phrases, and Tristram and Walter, both fascinated by the abstractions of philosophy, provide us repeatedly with instances of this all too human propensity.

The second abuse, "inconstancy in the use of [words]," is not less common: "And yet in arguings and learned contests, the same sort of proceedings passes commonly for wit and learning; but to me it appears a greater dishonesty than the misplacing of counters in the casting up a debt" (II.III.x.5;126). The novel abounds in relevant examples, for Tristram's use of pun and innuendo is typical of the wit's attempt to confuse and involve his audience. And Walter, as the rhetorician, must rely on such sleight-of-hand tricks. Fortunately, he is not always as obvious in his procedures as when he rejects at one point the plainness of Erasmus' argument and, seeking a greater complexity to take its place, he changes a Latin word completely by exchanging one of its letters for another: "See, my dear brother *Toby*, how I have mended the sense.——But you have marr'd a word, replied my uncle *Toby*" (III.xxxvii.230). What is explicit here is implied in learned conversations throughout the novel.

The third abuse is an extension of the second, sharing with it the force of deliberate action: *"Thirdly,* another abuse of language is an *affected obscurity*; by either applying old words to new and unusual significations; or introducing new and ambiguous terms, without defining either; or else putting them so together, as may confound their ordinary meaning" (II.III.x.6;126). Walter and Tristram are able practitioners of this technique. Indeed, it is the cornerstone of Tristram's narrative style, as the following admonition to Madam might suggest. It is the response to Toby's surprising but harmless comment "I wish, Dr. *Slop* . . . you had seen what prodigious armies we had in Flanders":

> In all disputes,——male or female,——whether for honour, for profit or for love,——it makes no difference in the case; ——nothing is more dangerous, madam, than a wish coming sideways in this unexpected manner upon a man: the safest way in general to take off the force of the wish, is, for the party wished at, instantly to get up upon his legs——and wish the *wisher* something in return, of pretty near the same value, ——so balancing the account upon the spot, you stand as you were——nay sometimes gain the advantage of the attack by it (III.i.157).

Conversation becomes a battleground. The object of meeting is the confusion of one's adversary. It provides the opportunity for an ironic comment that might well bewilder everyone but oneself, as when Walter, speaking of Toby's adventure in romance, replaces the word "passion" with the word "ass": "Well! dear brother *Toby,* said my father, upon his first seeing him after he fell in love——and how goes it with your AsSE?" (VIII.xxxii.584). As Tristram explains, ". . . it was not only a laconick way of expressing——but of libelling, at the same time, the desires and appetites of the lower part of us" (VIII.xxxi.584). Typically, Toby's inability to interpret Walter's figurative language maintains and even encourages the reader's doubts about the level of reality on which the novel is functioning.

Locke's fourth abuse of language is shared by all system-builders. It is parodied in Sterne's vignettes of academicians, and it is always exemplified by Walter: *"Fourthly,* Another great abuse of words, is the *taking them for things.* . . . To this abuse these men are most subject who must confine their thoughts to any one system, and give themselves up into a firm belief of the perfection of any received hypothesis: whereby they come to be persuaded that the terms of that sect are so suited to the nature of things, that they perfectly correspond with their real existence" (II.III.x.14;132). The fifth abuse is closely related: "the setting (of words) in the place of things which they do or can by no means signify" (II.III.x.17;135). Examples of both abound in the satiric digressions and, within the story, find utterance principally again through Walter. His conviction about the actual dwelling place of the soul is typical. It is a conviction which stimulates, in turn, his interest in obstetrical techniques: "What, therefore, seem'd the least liable to objections of any, was, that the chief sensorium, or head-quarters of the soul, and to which place all intelligences were referred, and from whence all her mandates were issued,——was in, or near, the cerebellum,——or rather some-where about the *medulla oblongata*, wherein it was generally agreed by *Dutch* anatomists, that all the minute nerves from all the organs of the seven senses concentered, like streets and winding alleys, into a square" (II.xix.149).

It is, however, Locke's sixth abuse of words which is responsible for the majority of pragmatic as well as academic misunderstandings. Locke describes this abuse as "proceeding upon the supposition that the Words we use have certain and evident Signification which other men cannot but understand" (II.III.ix.22;140). He goes on to explain that "the multiplication and obstinacy of disputes, which have so laid waste the intellectual world, is owing to nothing more than to this ill use of words. . . . the most I can find that the contending learned men of different parties do, in their arguings one with another is, that they speak different languages" (II.III.x.22; 142). In this category can be placed those misunderstandings which are due in *Tristram Shandy* to the literalization of figurative meaning: ". . . ——did ever a poor unfortunate man, brother *Toby*, cried my father, receive so many lashes?——The most I ever saw given, quoth my uncle *Toby*, . . . was to a grenadier, I think in *Makay's* regiment" (IV.iii.274). A similar miscalculation follows Walter's explanation of his reasons for considering the use of auxiliary verbs to be basic to all education.

> You excite my curiosity greatly, said *Yorick*.
> For my own part, quoth my uncle *Toby*, I have given it up.
> ——The *Danes*, an' please your honour, quoth the corporal, who were on the left at the siege of *Limerick*, were all auxiliaries. (V.xlii.405)

Sterne indicates, with great insight, the importance of "set" in interpretation. Preoccupied as he is with the circumstances of his own experience, every individual draws his response from unique associations which determine the accuracy and limitations of his understanding. Thus, when Walter asks what Dr. Slop's business is in the kitchen, after the delivery of his son, Trim replies: "He is busy, an' please your honour . . . in making a bridge" (III.xxiii.206). Trim means that the Doctor is attempting to construct a support for the infant's nose. But Toby, because of the intensity of his obsession, decides immediately that the bridge in question is the one so sorely needed as a replacement in his fortifications.

We find another example of the intransigence of association in connection with the Widow Wadman's anxious inquiries about "where" Toby received his wound. While she would like the afflicted area of his body to be specifically—even physically—identified, his thoughts lie exclusively with his map. It is for this reason that he can graciously assure her that "you shall lay your finger upon the place" (IX.xx.624), and it is thus that she is so cruelly deluded.

The following interchange between Yorick and Toby is less protracted but equally jolting: "——But you forget the great *Lipsius*, quoth *Yorick*, who composed a work the day he was born;——They should have wiped it up, said my uncle *Toby*, and said no more about it" (VI.ii.411–12).

The point is always the same: that all language is as susceptible to interpretation as the emptiest sound and the most ambiguous exclamation. When Phutatorius screams "Zounds!" in response to the sudden and surprising presence of a hot chestnut inside his breeches, individual predispositions give to his exclamation of pain technical, rhetorical, medical, and social explanations (IV.xxvii.318–19). It is neither the word itself nor the intention of the speaker that determines meaning. It is rather the state of mind of the auditor. Yorick's observation in *A Sentimental Journey* about the incompatibility of travel and communication suggests a metaphor that has a general application in the earlier novel: ". . . from the want of languages, connections and dependencies, and from the difference in educations, customs, and habits, we lie under so many impediments in communicating our sensations out of our own sphere, as often amount to a total impossibility" (p. 601). The uniqueness of each man's experience and the eccentricities of his personality make him always a traveler in a strange land and make of each man he encounters a probable alien.

Locke's optimistic hope is that a purposeful attempt at precise definition of terms will illuminate the obscurities of language and ameliorate the difficulties of communication. Sterne, whose concern is the language of common speech rather than the more exacting formulations of scientific investigation, anticipates some of the obstacles that the spontaneous flow of thought and conversation present to the painstaking procedures of verbal and conceptual analysis. As always the fault lies with the ascendancy of emotion and intuition over reasoned response. Sterne emphasizes the importance of implied meaning—conveyed by nuances of tone, gesture, and expression—analyzable on a psychological rather than on a linguistic level. Thus, we have the suggestiveness of Toby's ejaculation, offered in response to Dr. Slop's admission of his church's acceptance of the seven sacraments: "Humph!——said my uncle *Toby*; tho' not accented as a note of acquiescence,——but as an interjection of that particular species of surprize, when a man, in looking into a drawer, finds more of a thing than he expected . . . Dr. *Slop*, who had an ear, understood my uncle *Toby* as well as if he had wrote a whole volume against the seven sacraments" (II.xvii.129). Sterne insists also upon the importance of understanding the individual's perspective before assigning descriptive words to his behavior, motivations, or values. For example:

> I could like, said my mother, to look through the key-hole, out of *curiosity*——Call it by its right name, my dear, quoth my father——
> *And look through the key-hole* as long as you will. (VIII. xxxv.594)

> My father was a gentleman of many virtues,——but he had a strong spice of that in his temper which might, or might not, add to the number.——'Tis known by the name of perseverance in a good cause,——and of obstinacy in a bad one. . . . (I.xvii.43)

In addition to its revelation of the resistance of association to the categories of definition, Sterne's treatment of Locke—indeed his general view of the effectuality of language—contains another, greater irony. If words are powerless to capture and convey the multiplicity of personality, they do wield a power of their own. The implied emotional content rather than the concrete meaning carries the force of a word—a force so strong that is is frequently described in physical terms. Thus Yorick speaks of directing "five words point blank to the heart": "As *Yorick* pronounced the word *point blank*, my uncle *Toby* rose up to say something upon projectiles——when a single word, and no more, uttered from the opposite side of the table, drew every one's ears towards it" (IV.xxvi.317). The word is "zounds." It is the expression of a physical sensation, and it acts as a physical stimulus.

Indeed, in many ways, *Tristram Shandy* can be read as a book about the power of the word. According to Sterne's view, language is in only the most limited sense a tool which can be mastered by the skillful. Rather, it is a part of man's natural environment, apart from and alien to himself. To the extent that it must exist beyond the powers of his immediate comprehension, it dominates him. To the extent that it is part of the objective world, only partially known, it exerts a force that he cannot control. In his handling of language, therefore, with its peculiar tension between the objective and subjective universes, Sterne reveals the greatest ambiguity of the empiricist's position.

The dominant place of language in Sterne's catalogue of determining forces is implied in the first incident of the novel. Mrs. Shandy's rude interruption of her husband's performance of his conjugal duties—"*Pray, my dear*, quoth my mother, *have you not forgot to wind up the clock?*" (I.i.5)—is held as the primary determination of Tristram's physical, emotional, psychological, and artistic life. Nor is this the only way in which Tristram is victimized by the power of the word. His baptism removes him from the perilous state of nature only to plunge him into the pre-ordained failure that is the concomitant of his name. Finally, it is his own preoccupation with language that determines the eccentric "nonstructure" of his work and makes of it the very antithesis of art.

Nor is Tristram the only one of the Shandys to endure the undermining effects of language. As we have seen, the form of Toby's life is a function of his defeat by words. Unable to articulate, he regresses to the playing of a game in which communication is unimportant. Walter, though more trusting of language, is no more successful. In conjunction with the theory of education which he describes in his *Tristrapædia*, he puts forth a theory of auxiliary

verbs. Not unlike Locke, he finds that his epistemology must be reduced to a theory of language, but the theory of language which he
advocates is diametrically opposed to that proposed by the philosopher. Walter propounds a self-defeating semanticism which has
astonishing parallels to the semantics of contemporary logic. According to this view it is the structure of language rather than its content
that is of primary importance. The contention of Toby and Trim
that they cannot describe an object which they have not seen
(V.xlii.406) is in line with Locke's position. But Walter is interested
in logical possibility rather than empirical fact. Discourse becomes a
rational exercise concerned with the conditional. If it obviates the
difficult ambiguities and subjective variations of conventional discourse, it also obviates the relevance of personal experience and the
possibilities of normative values. It substitutes the bare bones of
form for the rich texture of meaning. The irony is clearly drawn. It
is also inescapable.

Finally, with his generous use of puns, innuendoes, and double
entendres—most of which are given some sexual relevance—Sterne
not only points up the ambiguity of language but ingeniously extends the classic battle between the instinct and the reason into the
area of semantics. In these groups of words the functioning of a
subversive, irrational, and associational force is demonstrated. It is
another instance of man's inability to restrict his thought to the
obvious simplicities of logical definition. In his brilliant symbology
of noses and in his briefer parable on the transformation of the word
"whiskers" (V.i.344–48), Sterne describes the metaphorical development of language (the process whereby meaning is exhausted
and re-created) and the independence of words from the reality of
the objects they describe: "Does not all the world know, said the
curate *d'Estella* at the conclusion of his work, that Noses ran the
same fate some centuries ago in most parts of *Europe*, which
Whiskers have now done in the kingdom of *Navarre*.——The evil
indeed spread no further then,——but have not beds and bolsters,
and night-caps and chamber-pots stood upon the brink of destruction ever since? Are not trouse, and placket-holes, and pump handles—and spigots and faucets, in danger still, from the same association?——Chastity, by nature the gentlest of all affections——give it
but its head——'tis like a ramping and a roaring lion" (V.i.347–48).
This is but another aspect of the hysteria of the Shandy world. In
a startling translation of the classical formulation, the word becomes

master, the source of creation, autonomous. The novel, which has communication as a dominant theme, sets out to describe man's various attempts to control his primary, ennobling instrument; ultimately, it chronicles his failure. The self-defeating form of the novel is the full expression of this irony.

Love and sexuality. If man's language is a function of one of his basic needs, the need for communication, his sexuality represents another. As a biological need which has instinct as its motivating power, it can be placed at the opposite end of the scale from the first, which satisfies and conforms to various social and psychological requirements and must therefore be subject to a process of learning. "Love" mediates between the two. It is, in effect, a socialization of instinct and an expression of man's desire to communicate. It can only be defined according to the values and demands of the particular society and the individual psychology. The relation of these to the unique situation and the universal predicament provided Sterne with another possibility for exposing character and elaborating upon his position of philosophical irony. Sterne's treatment of this theme has always incurred the vociferous opposition of the pure-hearted: an opposition which reached its peak with the Victorians, but persists, although more subtly phrased, into our own time. Alice Fredman is a recent proponent of this point of view: "Diderot regards the sexual urge as a very important part of human nature, whereas Sterne is either apprehensive of it or thinks that it is funny,—and somewhat improper. . . . While Sterne's insinuations are quite clear, his use of a thinly veiled approach coupled with suggestions of indecorum, would seem to reflect the author's inhibitions."[6] Sterne's view of sexuality was actually much more enlightened and comprehensive than this statement implies, and what might appear to be derived from inhibition or prurience seems more likely to be an appropriate part of the total artistic and philosophical vision.[7]

First of all, Sterne sets out to indicate the way in which all the activities most basic to the human economy are related linguistically and symbolically to the sexual function. Man is preoccupied with his body, and all his aspirations, all his attempts to escape his physical

6. *Diderot and Sterne*, p. 80.
7. Robert Alter explores the connection of Sterne's use of sex as a motif with his thematic interest in communication in his book *Rogue's Progress*, p. 317.

needs, are doomed to failure. We have just seen the way in which language is created anew, developing through slang and double entendres the sexual implications of a word. Of course, much of this "bawdy" can be traced to the associations induced by the physical objects themselves in an interplay of the mind and its environment which was described by Sterne before it was treated systematically by Freud. The frequent use of military objects in this way is effective in its relation both to theme and character.[8] Thus, Trim falls in the fossé when showing Bridget the fortifications they have so carefully constructed, only to have her later fall against and destroy their "bridge." Walter capitalizes upon the implications of the incidents by exploiting the suggestiveness of military tactics and instruments—all under the guise of history: ". . . my father would exhaust all the stores of his eloquence (which indeed were very great) in a panegyric upon the BATTERING-RAMS of the ancients,——the VINEA which *Alexander* made use of at the siege of *Tyre*.——He would tell my uncle *Toby* of the CATAPULTAE of the *Syrians* which threw such monstrous stones so many hundred feet, and shook the strongest bulwarks from their very foundation;——he would go on and describe the wonderful mechanism of the BALLISTA, which *Marcellinus* makes so much rout about,——the terrible effects of the PYRABOLI, ——which cast fire,——the danger of the TEREBRA and SCORPIO, which cast javelins,——But what are these, he would say, to the destructive machinery of corporal Trim?—Believe me, brother *Toby*, no bridge, or bastion, or sally port that ever was constructed in this world, can hold out against such artillery" (III.xxiv.211).

All of Toby's talk of "curtins," "horn-works," "ravelins," "half-moons," "covered ways," "counter-guards," and "ditches" is made the more interesting by the relation, already discussed, of his hobby-horse to his wound and his repressed sexuality. Furthermore, Trim, in his more open way, expounds picturesquely upon the conventional comparison of love and war—a comparison which does, incidentally, express perfectly his own attitude. He looks upon both activities with a relaxed acceptance of *their* naturalness and *his* duty: "All womankind . . . from the highest to the lowest, an' please your honour, love jokes; the difficulty is to know how they chuse to have them cut; and there is no knowing that, but by trying as we do with

---

8. Sigurd Burckhardt, *"Tristram Shandy*'s Law of Gravity," discusses the relation of military language and objects to sexuality.

our artillery in the field, by raising or letting down their breeches, till we hit the mark" (IX.viii.609). Concretizing the traditional association of death with copulation, Sterne connects the two experiences in his account of the death of Le Fever's wife (VI.vii.423), and in Walter's description of the death of Cornelius Gallus, which is introduced in order to prove "how little alteration in great men, the approaches of death have made" (V.iii.356).

Nor are the investigations of reason held to be free of sexual connotation. For example, Walter's fascination with nose-lore has its definite ambiguity, as do his "beds of justice." Indeed, the relation of his love of the intellectual and his more repressed physical drive is made quite explicit: ". . . my father clapp'd both his hands upon his cod-piece, which was a way he had when any thing hugely tickled him . . ." (VII.xxvii.514). Religious motives are similarly revealed to have sexual roots. Walter's response to the story of Saint Maxima's pilgrimage belies the orientation forced upon him by his wife's frigidity, while it also suggests a possible motivation of the mystic. "And what did she get by it? said my uncle *Toby*——What does any woman get by it? said my father——MARTYRDOME; replied the young *Benedictine* . . ." (VII.xxvii.514). The hypothetical interests of the religieuse in sexuality is reiterated throughout the novel. It is satirized at some length in "Slawkenbergius's Tale," which emphasizes the sexual preoccupations shared (although variously treated) by the practitioners of the "learned" professions. It is an acute anticipation of the possibilities of sublimation.

In his handling of Tristram's constant allusions, innuendoes, and double-entendres, Sterne also makes a more general comment about the attitudes and defenses of the more pedestrian spectator. By carefully maintaining an ambiguity of tone and reference, Sterne manages to implicate and bewilder "Sir" and "Madam," unmasking prudery, encouraging curiosity, and breaking down the inevitably shabby defense.

As we have seen, Walter, Tristram, and Toby are representatives of three distinct modes of apprehension. These modes are applied significantly to their sexual problems which, while peculiar to their own personal circumstances, are given a broader reference.[9] It is important to remember that the Shandy men all share some specific

9. A. R. Towers, "Sterne's Cock and Bull Story," discusses some of these same ideas, examining them in a similar perspective.

handicap which frustrates their sexuality. For Toby and Tristram the handicap consists of a physical disability. Their situations, however, are not as simple as they do at first seem. Neither is Sterne's intention. Disability is surrounded by ambiguity and given a social reference which negates the possibility of appraising the objective condition of each man. The nature and extent of Tristram's incapacity is always kept purposely vague. Innuendoes and double-entendres are the principal means used to convey an impression of his sterility. The two critical incidents which are suggested as determinate in Tristram's sexual development are the crushing of his nose at birth and the falling of the window-sash. With regard to the first, we have only Dr. Slop's suggestion about the danger of forceps delivery, offered before Tristram's birth: ". . . ——'tis a point very difficult to know,——and yet of the greatest consequence to be known;—— because, Sir, if the hip is mistaken for the head,——there is a possibility (if it is a boy) that the forceps* * * * * * * * * . . ." (III.xvii.187–88). Other than this, there is the association that is developed throughout the book with the word "nose" as well as Toby's association of the bridge that Dr. Slop constructs for the infant's broken nose with the "draw-bridge" that Trim has been responsible for destroying. Actually there is no reason at all to question Trim's description of the event: no reason at all, but for the double-entendres it contains: "God bless your honour, cried *Trim*, 'tis a bridge for master's nose.——In bringing him into the world with his vile instruments, he has crush'd his nose, *Susannah* says, as flat as a pancake to his face, and he is making a false bridge with a piece of cotton and a thin piece of whalebone out of *Susannah*'s stays, to raise it up" (III.xxvii.214–15).

Greater ambiguity but no more damning evidence is offered in explanation of the results of the window-sash episode. That Tristram has been unexpectedly circumcised is clear, but "If it be but right done" (V.xxvii.384) remains obscure. Walter's responses to Toby's and Yorick's anxious questions are models of historical reference and evasion.

> But is the child, cried my uncle *Toby*, the worse?——The *Troglodytes* say not, replied my father.——And your theologists, *Yorick*, tell us——Theologically? said *Yorick*,——or speaking after the manner of apothecaries?——statesmen?—— or washer-women?

——I'm not sure, replied my father,——but they tell us, brother *Toby*, he's the better for it. (V.xxviii.386)

Susannah's report might be the result of panic. It might be a common prejudice against the unusual, or it might be a valid response to a serious situation. Immediately after the accident she cries (is it literal or figurative; is it a matter of punctuation?): "——Nothing is left,——cried *Susannah*,——nothing is left——for me, but to run my country——" (V.xvii.376). And later she characterizes the affair as the "murder" of Tristram (V.xviii.376). Nor is Yorick's comment "You have cut off spouts enow" (V.xviii.382) less misleading. Furthermore, actuality becomes unimportant beside the report which Dr. Slop gives out. Once the rumour is established, fact itself could not controvert it:

> I would shew him publickly, said my uncle *Toby*, at the market cross.
> ——'Twill have no effect, said my father. (IV.xiv.433)

Walter's final solution, which is to put the boy in breeches, is only a way of obscuring the real problem, and caters to the society's interest and belief in "appearance." Just as language becomes in the Shandy world an autonomous, creative force, so does the appearance (the conjecture, the interpretation) displace physical fact. One feels that Tristram has been rendered impotent, if not by the actual effects of physical circumstances, then by effects as they are imagined by society.

> ——Do, my dear *Jenny*, tell the world for me, how I behaved under one [of the disasters of my life], the most oppressive of its kind which could befall me as a man, proud, as he ought to be, of his manhood——
> 'Tis enough, said'st thou, coming close up to me, as I stood with my garters in my hand, reflecting on what had *not* pass'd. (VII.xxix.517–18)

Furthermore, his impotence seems also to be a function of his aestheticism—a concern for the emotional sensation, rather than the physical experience. Henri Fluchère makes an interesting comparison between the "coarseness" of *Tristram Shandy* and the delicacy of *A Sentimental Journey*. "Ce n'est pas le fait sexuel qui domine, c'est la conscience d'une feminité, avec ses attributs de grace, et de perversité delicat, bref d'une presence lascive impossible à situer dans la maison des Shandy." And later: "La grossièreté robuste du monde Shandéen fait place aux joies subtiles de la préfiguration des delices qu'un erotisme expert arrête avant la consummation" (p. 444). Fluchère's distinction is, of course, correct, but it is important to note the transitional role which Tristram plays in comparison with the sentimentality of the later work. Both Yorick and Tristram have an aesthetic sensibility which demands satisfaction in a world of imaginative constructs. Tristram insists upon the platonic nature of his relationships, and, significantly, at the end of the seventh volume, he specifically rejects the possibility of love in favor of art (VII.xliii.538). His interest is in romance rather than in sexuality.

The outline of Toby's situation is strikingly similar. For example, we are led to believe that Toby dwells in a world of illusion that has all of the validity of a more concrete reality. The extent of his wound is ambiguously referred to, but here we have Trim's unequivocal report to Bridget to assure us that Toby's manhood, while threatened, was not destroyed.

> . . . in this cursed trench, Mrs. *Bridget*, quoth the Corporal, taking her by the hand, did he receive the wound which crush'd him so miserably *here*——In pronouncing which he slightly press'd the back of her hand towards the part he felt for——and let it fall.
>
> We thought, Mr. *Trim*, it had been more in the middle—— said Mrs. *Bridget*——
>
> That would have undone us for ever——said the Corporal.
>
> ——And left my poor mistress undone too—said *Bridget*. (IX.xxviii.639)

Toby's impotence, which can probably be more aptly described as total lack of interest, is psychologically and not physically derived. Thus Tristram speaks in the following way of Toby's "modesty of nature": "——tho' I correct the word nature, for this reason, that I may not prejudge a point which must shortly come to a hearing; and that is, Whether this modesty of his was natural or acquir'd" (I.xxi. 66). In Toby's case, society, in the person of the Widow Wadman, introduces the force of opinion and causes a kind of paralysis. But, in addition to this, and perhaps of greater importance, Toby's emotionality must be taken into account. There is an element of the paradoxical and the perverse about Toby's response to the Widow Wadman, much as there is in his response to war. Their story is an anti-romance in which the roles of the lovers are reversed, the love unconsummated, and the ending disastrous. The affair is itself suggestive of sterility, covering as it does a period of nine months, its offspring stillborn (III.xxiv.209). In effect, an atrophy of sexual feeling is involved. Just as his attitude toward war is illusory—a response to superficial values and complex mechanisms—so too is his attitude toward physical love an escape into illusion. He can summon some response to the ideal and he can pursue the proscribed forms of procedure, but the motivating energy of it all—the sexual urge—is completely overlooked. When faced with it he is shocked and repelled. His only possible response is to withdraw completely and irrevocably into the world of unreality which is emotionally acceptable.

Finally, we must consider the parallel that can be drawn between Walter's circumstances and those of Tristram and Toby. Walter too suffers from a sexual wound that renders him partially impotent. His indifference is its symptom. It is a wound that society has helped to fashion in the sexual fear, repression, and passivity presented to him in the person of his wife. Furthermore, there is reflected in Walter's response to his conjugal situation the normal attitude of the man of reason toward that which threatens the order and logic of his private intellectual universe. Walter's choice of words, in this description of error, would seem to belie his position: "The laws of nature will defend themselves;——but error ——(he would add, looking earnestly at my mother)——error, Sir, creeps in thro' the minute holes, and small crevices, which human nature leaves unguarded" (II.xix.146). The irrational and emotional aspects of sexual indulgence controvert everything in which Walter believes. The most careful planning, the most cautious attempts to control the force of instinct, cannot succeed. The misfortunes connected with Tristram's conception are the proof. And because in Walter's experience there are no compensations for the disadvantages, he reaches a position of extreme protest, as close to withdrawal as he can come without denying completely his biological nature. Speaking of Toby's disillusionment he sets about demonstrating to Yorick "not only, 'That the devil was in women, and that the whole of the affair was lust;' but that every evil and disorder in the world, of what kind or nature soever, from the first fall of *Adam*, down to my uncle *Toby*'s (inclusive) was owing one way or other to the same unruly appetite" (IX.xxxii.644).

It seems that it is only on Trim's level (and this raises a question about Sterne's implied distinction among social classes) that sexuality can be openly accepted, encouraged, and enjoyed. The comparison between uncle Toby's affair with the Widow Wadman and Trim's encounter with Bridget contrasts enthusiasm with passivity, spontaneity with deviousness, simplicity with complexity: "Indeed in my uncle Toby's case there was a strange and unaccountable concurrence of circumstances which insensibly drew him in, to lay siege to that fair and strong citadel.——In Trim's case there was a concurrence of nothing in the world but of him and Bridget in the kitchen" (III.xxiv.208). Toby and Tristram withdraw to the illusions of the unconsummated romance. Walter chooses the safety of systematic procedures which parade beneath the flag of reason. All are able to find some comfort in the sentimental relationship possible among themselves: the nonverbal empathic meetings that take place at various times, in various combinations, and include Toby, Trim, Walter, Yorick, and Tristram. Such meetings are safe because they exclude the necessity of sexuality. And they are beneficial in their humanitarian sentiment and intention. They become the foundation of *A Sentimental Journey* and are characterized by Sterne in a letter which explains his purpose in writing his last work. "I told you my design in it was to teach us to love the world and our fellow creatures better than we do—so it runs most upon those gentler passions and 'affections,' which aid so much to it."[10]

A sense of the unnatural remains—a consequence of the frustration born of the lack of communication. But Sterne successfully incorporates this perverse sexuality into his broad ironic pattern. The subject of numerous conversations, the object of great interest, the focus of much activity, sex remains largely theoretical. On the Shandys' level of existence, it ceases to be the natural expression of an instinctual drive and becomes the symbol of the incompatibility of illusion and reality. The potentiality of sexual satisfaction is an incapacitating wound, an inescapable reminder of animality to a man who aspires to the possession of an ideal. It is the reminder of a physical fact which defies analysis and must simply be accepted. It

10. "To Mrs. William James," (November 12, 1767), *Letters*, p. 401.

is the irony of the epistemologist's position. The truth is irrelevant even in the rare cases when it can be known. It is only opinion that is important, for it is only opinion that has its effect upon human affairs. It is opinion, not fact, let us remember, that causes the undoing of Tristram and Toby. The alternatives are simple: escape or spontaneous acceptance. The Shandys escape, each withdrawing to his own world of illusion. Trim accepts. The reader is left in the position of most men, faced with a mass of conjecture, fact, and possibility. His attention is demanded, his curiosity is aroused, but the attempts of reason are doomed to failure.

Death and the tragi-comedy of life.—Death is another of *Tristram Shandy*'s major themes. In its treatment, Sterne focuses his sense of the tragi-comic experience of life. Contrasting the universal presence of the transitory with the complex meaning of death in the lives of the living, Sterne creates a concept that is as elusive as it is subtle. In defense of Sterne's seriousness we have only to remember the way in which the transitory is given meaning through the association of Yorick and Hamlet: this is an association that ennobles despite its ironic overtones. Or we can consider the genuine brilliance of Trim's oration with its concrete metaphor of death, or Tristram's vision of Uncle Toby's death, which in no way discredits the validity of an intense emotional response. There is also Tristram's evocation and poetic speech to Jenny, which places her within the ever-changing cycle of human life (IX.viii.610–11), and the sentimental note of Le Fever's story, which is sounded with considerable, if obvious, force.

Indeed, it is interesting to note that the only death in *Tristram Shandy* which is not handled with an appropriate solemnity is that of Tristram's elder brother, Bobby. Here Sterne is able to elicit a strong response to the macabre in the way in which the news is delivered to those most interested. For the reader, who has prior knowledge of the event, as well as certain conventional expectations, the process is painful and even shocking. The comic misunderstandings of Walter and Toby, the fumbling steps taken by the mind in its anxiety to comprehend, and the vagaries and incapacities of language are given a new dimension: "——he's gone! said my uncle *Toby*.——Where——Who? cried my father.——My nephew, said my uncle *Toby*.——What——without leave——without money——without governor? cried my father in amazement.

No:———he is dead, my dear brother, quoth my uncle *Toby*.———
Without being ill? cried my father again.———I dare say not, said my
uncle *Toby*, in a low voice, and fetching a deep sigh from the bottom of his heart, he has been ill enough, poor lad! I'll answer for
him———for he is dead" (V.ii.350).

Mrs. Shandy's situation is equally ironic. Tristram first chooses
to leave her eavesdropping on Walter's irrelevant oration while he
describes the reception of the news "below stairs." When he picks
her up again it is only to report the incongruity of her interchange
with her husband.

> I have friends———I have relations,———I have three desolate
> children,"———says *Socrates*.———
> ———Then, cried my mother, opening the door,———you have
> one more, Mr. *Shandy*, than I know of.
> By heaven! I have one less,———said my father, getting up
> and walking out of the room. (V.xiii.370)

The fact that Mrs. Shandy's position of concerned and misinformed
ignorance is placed before and after the kitchen scene adds contrast to the spectrum of responses with which Sterne concerns himself, and Sterne's decision to end the scene inconclusively, without
indicating the extent of Mrs. Shandy's enlightenment, has strong
dramatic impact.

Nor is the kitchen scene (V.vii.359–62), so rich in comic effects,
completely lacking in a sense of the *lachrimae rerum*. The universality of the phenomenon which Sterne describes does have its
poignant aspect. It is a scene which underlines the inextricable connection of human values and interests with the largely incomprehensible fact of death. It is another example of the way in which
the mind creates its reality—the totality of its illusions—from the
recognizable elements of its own environment. Death, like language
and sexuality, is the formless material of life which is given shape
by the limited powers and associations of every individual. For
Susannah, Bobby's death means the acquisition of Mrs. Shandy's
green satin nightgown, a more seductive object for her than for her
mistress. The foolish scullion's simple response, "So am not I," is
the primary affirmation of ego. For Obadiah, the death represents
the end of indecision. He can now "stub the ox-moor"; for Trim it
is a glorious opportunity for the instinctual philosopher and orator.

Finally, for Tristram, Bobby's death means the possibility of establishing a position of importance for himself. "From this moment I am to be considered as heir-apparent to the *Shandy* family——and it is from this point properly, that the story of my LIFE and OPINIONS sets out; with all my hurry and precipitation I have but been clearing the ground to raise the building" (IV.xxxii.336).

What Ernest Dilworth refers to as the most "sprightly vaudeville of lamentation as may be found in literature"[11] is actually an acute insight into one of the most ironic and tragi-comic propensities of the human psyche. That which he describes as Tristram's "shocking disrespect for death" (p. 19) is actually an accurate recognition of the possibility that death can enrich life by simplifying it. Thus Sterne presents each successive family calamity as an opportunity for terminating concern over the last. The error of Tristram's christening takes precedence over the ill omen of his nose-flattening. The problem of renaming him is replaced by that of Aunt Dinah's legacy, which forces Walter to decide between the renovation of his ox-moor and sending Bobby on a Grand Tour. Bobby's death, of course, solves this dilemma, and Walter's grief is assuaged by his immersion in the *Tristrapædia*, which introduces its own conflict between real and artistic time. Thus Tristram asks with validity: "What is the life of man! Is it not to shift from side to side?—— from sorrow to sorrow?——to button up one cause of vexation! ——and unbutton another!" (IV.xxxi.336). Once again, Sterne answers that in the face of the unknown and unmanageable, man's only recourse is to those private illusions built by his particular mode of perception. It is only to be expected, therefore, that Walter, Toby, and Tristram should respond in basically the same ways to death as they do to language and to sexuality. Walter embraces the formality of rhetoric, the security of history. He escapes by placing the formless and frightening phenomenon in familiar categories, applying to it the familiar formulations. Sound is substituted for the feeling that would defy reason. Reason is applied subjectively, in the interests of personality rather than objective truth. It is still for Walter an adjunct of imagination.

Another kind of irony accompanies Toby's attitude toward death. We have already considered his paradoxical acceptance of the horrors of war, his escape into the simplistic heroic values of child-

---

11. *The Unsentimental Journey of Laurence Sterne*, p. 17.

hood and the beneficial sublimation of play. But in his sentimental response to the individual fatality—whether it be the captivity of a fly or the death of Le Fever—we are given a new insight. Toby's attitude is revealed to be a slightly exaggerated version of a universal paradox: those who cannot mourn for multitudes can still sympathize warmly with the individual predicament. It is a statement about the quality of "sympathy" and a fundamental irony of the emotions.

Tristram's escape is apparent, of course, in the method he uses to reverse the effects of his more pathetic scenes: in his use of language and the juxtaposition of situation and comment. Most imaginative of all is his use in the seventh volume of the "Grand Tour" as a metaphor for the flight from death. It is a metaphor that is developed on both serious and comic levels and is given a brilliantly ironic twist. Never lapsing into self-pity and maintaining always a tone of joviality, Tristram is able to convey through the details of the chase a sense of feverish activity which has its ominous aspects. Similarly, his humour will frequently exhibit a grimness and morbidity which emphasize both the seriousness of his situation and the brave, objective humour he is able to sustain.

Even more interesting than Tristram's tonal balance is the ironic turn which he gives to his metaphorical journey. While the Grand Tour is a flight from and toward death, Tristram imaginatively perceives the way in which it can be conversely treated as a paradigm of the journey through life: a journey in which the awareness of fatality sharpens the recognition of human values. Hans Meyerhoff, in his discussion of time and literary themes, comments upon this positive meaning of the journey: "Both ceaseless striving and activity are ways of counteracting the negative implications of the inexorable and undeniable progression of time toward death. . . . The pursuit, or the pleasure of pursuit, has intrinsic value because it is oblivious of the goal pursued or the value of the goal; it is oblivious also of the ultimate goal set for every pursuit in life, namely death."[12] Tristram himself specifically formulates this idea: ". . . so much of motion, is so much of life, and so much of joy——and that to stand still, or get on but slowly, is death and the devil——" (VII.xiii.493). The temporal scheme of the novel represents yet another version of the same self-defeating, yet curiously successful, movement.

12. *Time in Literature*, p. 70.

Finally, it must be remembered that Tristram's discussion of the Grand Tour is also a revelation of the dearth of meaningful values in the activities of most lives. As he facetiously explains: " *'Make them like unto a wheel'* is a bitter sarcasm, as all the learned know, against the *grand tour"* (VII.xiii.492). Thus Tristram spurns the superficiality of sight-seeing and conventional social intercourse, and he finally withdraws completely, denying even the innocent temptations of Nanette so that he may write his book (VII.xliii.538). Presumably, then, his Grand Tour ends with a retreat into the possibilities of the imagination: a positive and constructive alternative to the fevered flight from death. It is, nevertheless, but another form of escape. Art, for all its timelessness, confronts him with a new set of temporal puzzles which are fascinating but insoluble.

The nightmare world of empiricism: the thematic presupposition.— It becomes increasingly clear that in accepting the implications of Locke's empiricism while rejecting his rationalizations and hopeful optimism, Sterne uncovers a nightmare world of alienation and absurdity. In considering man as a spiritual and physical being, capable of communication and thought, Sterne finds language most effective when it is inarticulate, spontaneity and sexuality expressed through the careful self-conscious constructs of sublimation, and knowledge of death restricted to the individual's concern for security and satisfaction. Upon everything Sterne places the stamp of inevitability, for he describes a world in which reason is the slave of imagination and reality a function of private illusion. He accepts only the intuitive, empathic response as a possible ground for order and understanding, but finds that this has no correlative in action. Illusion must constantly collide with a perverse, mysterious, and hostile environment. It is an alien world in which each instrument of perception and interpretation is unique, and it is a cruel world in which every man's life appears in some way trivial and eccentric to others though it is of dominant and all-engrossing interest to himself. It is, in brief, a world without absolutes; in such a world there cannot be even a simplicity of irony, for the terms of the ironic equation are not stable.

Sterne relentlessly questions Locke's belief that reason is capable of searching out and stringently defining moral standards of behavior which will then impose an imperative upon action. It is the ego which is supreme in judgment: the ego which does not see the self as it is measured by the universe, but rather sees the universe as it is reflected in the self. It is thus that the inversion of the great and the small, the important and the trivial, takes place. Tristram draws a generalization from the fact that his own digressive technique was suggested by a consideration of the nature of the earth's rotation: ". . . I believe the greatest of our boasted improvements and discoveries have come from such trifling hints" (I.xxii.73). And Dr. Slop becomes so involved in the immediate problem of undoing the knots in his instrument bag that he completely subverts the ultimate purpose of his profession. The trivial takes the place of the crucial, and God himself is made a party to it. " 'Tis God's mercy, quoth he, (to himself), that Mrs. *Shandy* has had so bad a time of it,——else she might have been brought to bed seven times told, before one half of these knots could have got untied" (III.ix.167).

Tristram's constant reduction of the abstract to the physical, another of the novel's themes, is a metaphor for the incompatibility of the inner man with the outer world, the incompatibility of the personal illusion with the obdurate external fact, the incompatibility of the perceived and the perceiver. While the individual mind is master of its possessor, it is hidden always from the understanding of the "other," and can be gleaned only by following circuitous external routes:

> . . . our minds shine not through the body, but are wrapt up here in a dark covering of uncrystalized flesh and blood; so that if we would come to the specifick characters of them, we must go some other way to work.
> Many, in good truth, are the ways which human wit has been forced to take to do this thing with exactness. (I.xxiii.75)

Tristram himself chooses to present the "minds" of his characters through an analysis of the "hobby-horse" which each one rides. His use of this metaphor and his development of it as a description of the growth of obsession is humorously and ambiguously suggestive of the rude encounter of the troubled self with the alien physical world to which it is attracted and from which it draws the pattern for its escape: "A man and his HOBBY-HORSE, tho' I cannot say that they act and re-act exactly after the same manner in which the soul and body do upon each other: Yet doubtless there is a communication between them of some kind, and my opinion rather is, that there is something in it more of the manner of electrified bodies,——and that by means of the heated parts of the rider, which come immediately into contact with the back of the HOBBY-HORSE.——By long journies and much friction, it so happens that the body of the rider is at length fill'd as full of HOBBY-HORSICAL matter as it can hold . . ." (I.xxiv.77). It follows, then, that the effect of an action will frequently turn out to be the opposite of what was intended, for intention can take into account only the subjective facts which stimulate it and not the objective world by which it is received. Thus, when Dr. Slop is confronted by the furiously galloping Obadiah, he piously crosses himself, only to find that the spiritual gesture has nothing to do with practical considerations. He loses his whip, his stirrup, his seat, and, finally, his presence of mind (II.ix.106). Similarly, it is Toby's benevolent hobby and Trim's devotion to the desires of his master that are found to be indirectly and unpredictably responsible for Tristram's circumcision.

The paradoxical relationship prevailing between public time and private time is but another expression of the dilemma of subjective meaning and objective truth. For example, Walter encounters the problem of coexisting temporal levels in his writing of the *Tristrapaedia*, which is constantly frustrated by the rate of Tristram's growth: ". . . he was three years and something more, indefatigably at work, and at last, had scarce compleated, by his own reckoning, one half of his undertaking: the misfortune was, that I was all that time totally neglected and abandoned to my mother; and what was almost as bad, by the very delay, the first part of the work, upon which my father had spent most of his pains, was rendered entirely useless,——every day a page or two became of no consequence——" (V.xvi.375). This is but another of the ways in which Walter feels himself thwarted and his power demeaned by indifferent forces that he can neither know nor control. As Tristram describes it, this discrepancy represents an almost classical predicament of suffering humanity. "——Certainly it was ordained as a scourge upon the pride of human wisdom, That the wisest of us all, should thus outwit ourselves, and eternally forego our purposes in the intemperate act of pursuing them" (V.xvi.375). It is once again the miserable fate of Sisyphus, shared by Toby, whose games of war and love must be played for their own sake without the possibility of fruition or completion, and by Tristram, who must face and be defeated by a multi-level temporality, represented by his readers, his characters, and himself: "I am this month one whole year older than I was this time twelve-month; and having got, as you perceive, almost into the middle of my fourth volume——and no farther than to my first day's life——'tis demonstrative that I have three hundred and sixty-four days more life to write just now, than when I first set out; so that instead of advancing, as a common writer, in my work with what I have been doing at it . . . at this rate I should just live 364 times faster than I should write——It must follow, an' please your worships, that the more I write, the more I shall have to write——and consequently, the more your worships read, the more your worships will have to read" (IV.xiii.285–86).

If the formalizations and inflexibility of the external environment seem to represent betrayals of personal integrity, then the formalizations projected by the individual represent, in turn, a betrayal of self. Tristram's diary supplies the peasant woman with adequate curl papers for her hair. Maria's pagan religion with its spontaneity and instinctual regard for human values has more validity than a formal Christianity with little regard for her difficulties. Walter's lecture on the value of radical heat and radical moisture as the basis of health (V.xxxiii.394) contains no more wisdom than Toby's interpretation of the phenomena as "a burning fever, attended with a most raging thirst" (V.xxxviii.399) or Trim's definition of the terms as "ditch water" and "burnt brandy" (V.xl.402). It is Sisyphus' absurd world: a comic world defined by mishap, ineptitude, and blundering, a world to which is added a profound dimension by the stubborn and, at times, noble persistence of its small heroes.

The Thematic Unity

The fascination of *Tristram Shandy* derives from its complexity: the levels on which it has been written and the levels on which it may be judged. The complexity is valid, for Sterne saw and attempted to communicate the erratic and the unpredictable in nature. Through Tristram he set out to convey the incapacities of art and the absurdity of man before the incomprehensible. With the structure of his work he suggested the elusiveness of the artistic truth. In all, he created a pattern of irony worthy of his own vision. Although his work cannot escape the appearance of the random, the incomplete, and the eccentric, like nature itself it hides the principle of its structure. The richness and ambiguity are there. The plan is present also.

We have seen that the structural unity of *Tristram Shandy* derives from Tristram. His associations as artist, biographer, and social critic are wide-ranging and inclusive—embracing even the associations of those characters whose thoughts and actions he has set out to describe. The tremendous latitude of the work's movement and the ambiguity of Tristram's tone combine, however, to create a generally confusing effect. When the novel is read as a study of self-alienation, this sense is dispelled and an awareness of an important direction and unity takes its place. One is no longer forced to adopt Tristram's faulty perspective. The point of view that is shared becomes Sterne's own.

The first six volumes of *Tristram Shandy* represent the hero's attempt to give an account of his life presented against the background of the familial and social milieu. As such, it becomes a history of isolation: a description of a child's conditioning through his systematic separation from an environment that can be logically explained or purposefully shaped. By extension, it is the history of the alienation of man from himself, his family, his friends, his social and professional peers. Abstractly, it tells of the separation of the body from the external world with which it is in contact, of the mind from its perceptual object, the word from its meaning, the feeling from its expression, the illusion from the reality. In the first six volumes we are introduced to the paradoxes of the empiricist's world. As we have seen, they are concerned with modes of perception, problems of communication, conflicts of love and sexuality, and the subjective apprehension of death. All are explored and applied by Tristram in his roles of artist, biographer, and social philosopher. The episodes in these volumes relate the chaotic collision of external forces that have determined his life (clocks, forceps, window sashes, and familial eccentricities) to artistic muddles of meaning and expression and the hypocritical confusion of social pretension and learned aspiration. All "digressions" are part of a broad plan which develops the novel's central theme, and even the longest of them, those which seem most to .threaten the tenuous continuity of the work, are found to have logic and validity in their reference to a more inclusive universe of values. Placed in the proper perspective, these extended digressions can all be shown to serve important unifying functions.

Trim's reading of one of Yorick's sermons (II.xvii.120–43) provides us with one of the two major examples from the first six volumes. The scene functions as a play-within-a-play, suggesting the thematic line of the novel as well as its technique. Trim's real relationship to his audience is a parallel of Tristram's relationship to his reader. Yorick stands behind the first as Sterne stands behind the second. An epistemological and aesthetic comment is offered as each of the characters projects himself into the sermon, which ultimately becomes an extension of them as they reveal their customary forms of response. The lack of understanding and absence of real communication, which is the result of their interaction, suggests dramatically the nature of one of the primary empiricist paradoxes.

The sermon takes as its text a passage from Hebrews 13:18: "For we trust we have a good conscience." Its theme is self-deception—a major theme of the novel as well. It analyzes the growth and acceptance of hypocrisy in the consciences of specific types of men. In its treatment of the Inquisition it indicates also the hypocrisy of social institutions: the paradox of cruelty committed in the name of Christianity, the betrayal of men and women by a system which has their service as its theoretical function.

The central irony of the scene lies, of course, in the sermon's ineffectuality: the way in which its point is demonstrated as its capacity for meaningful expression is disproved. The moral of the sermon is offered in this passage:

> So that if you would form a just judgment of what is of infinite importance to you not to be misled in,——namely, in what degree of real merit you stand either as an honest man, an useful citizen, a faithful subject to your king, or a good servant to your God,——call in religion and morality.—— Look,——What is written in the law of God?——How readest thou?——Consult calm reason and the unchangeable obligations of justice and truth;——what say they?
>
> "Let CONSCIENCE determine the matter upon these reports; ——and then if thy heart condemns thee not, which is the case the Apostle supposes,——the rule will be infallible. . . .". (II.xvii.132–33)

In response to the suggestion, "consult calm reason and the unchangeable obligations of justice and truth," Dr. Slop falls asleep.

Walter is hardly more attentive to the sermon's message. He is pre-occupied instead with the style of its author and the technique of its orator. Not surprisingly, Trim's and Toby's interest is in the military strategy suggested by the fictional "characters" which the sermon analyzes, and because of their humanitarian sympathies, it is only to them that Yorick's meaning can be communicated. They respond to the particular example which can be assimilated into the limited patterns of their experience rather than to an abstract principle for which they have no coordinates.

Trim's reading of the sermon is perhaps most valuable in the novel's structure for its dramatic development of character. The brilliance of "Slawkenbergius's Tale" (IV.245–71), however, lies in its pre-sentation of the novel's formal and thematic ironies. While seeming at superficial glance to be a whimsical romp generally irrelevant to the work as a whole, it actually represents an opportunity for Tris-tram to apply his triple function to a consideration of the paradoxes of empiricism: the modes of perception, the use of language, the atti-tudes of sexuality, and the position of alienation. In this great comic allegory, Diego, the hero, stands as a surrogate for Tristram. The identification is suggested by the association in preceding chapters of the crushing of Tristram's nose with the tale of Diego's journey, and is implemented, in the succeeding volume, by Tristram's un-expected circumcision. Growing out of a simple pun, the allegory becomes a version of sexual obsession as well as a compendium of the personal and social evils and confusions which invade Tristram's life.

On the most obvious level, "Slawkenbergius's Tale" is a satire of learned wit, directing its attack against all system-builders and pre-tenders to the absolute. Tristram the social critic is able to bring together the representatives of all philosophical positions, parodying the language and methods of rationalists, empiricists, and logicians alike, as the reality of the stranger's nose is variously questioned. Significantly, although the reality of the physical feature would seem to be an unequivocal matter of fact, it is perceived with as many variations as there are observers: ". . . ——in a word, each *Stras-burger* came crouding for intelligence——and every *Strasburger* had the intelligence he wanted" (IV.257). While the ignorant perceive the object of their interest in accordance with their prejudices and expectations and then describe it metaphorically—the trumpeter's wife uses her husband's trumpet as a visual aid (IV.256)—the learned use it as a beginning point from which they might pursue the investigations most relevant to their particular studies. Thus, the medical doctors get into a heated but irrelevant debate about wens and œdematous swellings (IV.257–59). The civil lawyers concern themselves not with the discovery of "truth" but rather with the continuation of controversy. To this end they prove that "the stranger's nose was neither true nor false" (IV.260). The metaphysicians, on the other hand, find that their disagreement about the reality and nature of the nose leads to an argument about the essence of God:

> This at once started a new dispute, which they pursued a great way upon the extent and limitation of the moral and natural attributes of God—That controversy led them naturally into *Thomas Aquinas*, and *Thomas Aquinas* to the devil.
>
> The stranger's nose was no more heard of in the dispute—— it just served as a frigate to launch them into the gulph of school-divinity,——and then they all sailed before the wind. (IV.264)

Tristram creates the image of a people driven and victimized by their attempts to rationalize. He creates a physical sense of striving, futility, and chaos; and here, as also in his language and images, there is a pervasive air of sexuality. Indeed, when viewed from another perspective, the subject of the "Tale" can be interpreted as a celebration of naturally expressed sexuality and an ironic appraisal of prudery. When examined in this way, the didacticism, scholasticism, and rhetorical formality become commentary on the nature of sublimation. The academic world is then a teetering superstructure built on the unrecognizedly dangerous foundation of sexual urge. The nuns, in whom frustration and sublimation are most intensively developed, become prominent victims of social disease with their "placket holes" and "buttered buns," their dreams, their wakefulness, their auto-eroticism (IV.253–55). The concern of the people over the size and general appearance of Diego's nose, the role of gossip and malicious rumor in establishing a general attitude toward it, and Diego's own self-consciousness and failure of performance despite his apparent capabilities all comprise a paradigm of Tristram's—and Toby's—situation. It is but another version of the sexual paradox, the conflict between the reality and the illusion, that we are given throughout the novel.

The ending of the "Tale" adds a final touch of mythic significance, for the fall of Strasburg is attributed by Slawkenbergius to the intensity of the townspeople's obsession. To this the entrance of the French should be attributed:

> ——The *French* indeed, who are ever upon the catch, when they saw *Strasburgers*, men, women, and children, all marched out to follow the stranger's nose——each man followed his own, and marched in.
>
> Trade and manufactures have decayed and gradually grown down ever since——but not from any cause which commercial heads have assigned; for it is owing to this only, that Noses have ever so run in their heads, that the *Strasburgers* could not follow their business. (IV.271)

Sexuality is thus humorously identified as a universally disruptive force which subverts rationality while providing a fundamental power. If it is responsible for motivating investigations and activities, it is responsible also for the lack of fulfillment which is derived from them. Sublimation is therefore an uneasy compromise for the insoluble conflict between natural response and social form.

There is still another level on which the tale functions and another conflict which it raises. This conflict is artistic and concerns itself with "literary" and "realistic" values, for "Slawkenbergius's Tale" is an anti-romance. Ostensibly it tells the story of the chaste Julia and the chivalric Diego, recounting their sad misunderstanding and parting and anticipating their eventual reconciliation after great trouble. In actuality, Diego's great nose stands between them, subverting all of the conventional aspects of the story, revealing the actual nature of the values which lie beneath the contrived form. Just as Diego's physical deformity flaws his otherwise noble appearance, so do the actual concerns of his romantic attachment reveal themselves in the words he speaks to the mule whom he has named after his beloved. The supremacy of the word is once again asserted, as the identities of the real beast and the idealized maiden become hopelessly confused.

> O Julia, my lovely Julia!——nay I cannot stop to let thee bite that thistle——that ever the suspected tongue of a rival

should have robbed me of enjoyment when I was upon the
point of tasting it.——

. . .

Poor devil, thou'rt sadly tired with thy journey!——Come
——get on a little faster——there's nothing in my cloak-bag
but two shirts——a crimson-sattin pair of breeches, and a
fringed——Dear Julia! (IV.252)

The poetic language of his "Ode" is similarly betrayed by the ambiguity of the word and the undeniable power of the thought.

Ode

Harsh and untuneful are the notes of love,
Unless my Julia strikes the key,
Her hand alone can touch the part,
Whose dulcet move-
-ment charms the heart,
and governs all the man with sympathetic sway.

(IV.269)

Setting out to record a romance, Tristram offers instead a parody
in this comic celebration of the phallus. It is a serious statement
about sexual motivation and a serious criticism of a conventional
literary form. The theme is played, with appropriate variations, in
all the romantic encounters of the novel. It is played in the account
of Uncle Toby's courtship of the Widow Wadman, which is clearly
linked in Tristram's mind with the love affair of Julia and Diego:

But in this clear climate of fantasy and perspiration, where
every idea, sensible and insensible, gets vent——in this land,
my dear *Eugenius*——in this fertile land of chivalry and romance, where I now sit, unskrewing my ink-horn to write my
Uncle *Toby*'s amours, and with all the meanders of Julia's
track in quest of her Diego, in full view of my study window
——if thou comest not and takest me by the hand——
What a work is it likely to turn out! (VIII.i.539)

"Slawkenbergius's Tale" is like the work that "turns out," and like
the larger work that contains them both: a fiction which is other than
what it seems, a form within a form, a denial of the conventional

appearance, a commitment to sophisticated truth and ironic complexity.

Volume VII, which has been read as a long and irrelevant digression, can be considered also as an appropriate transitional section which offers another interesting insight into the nature of art. Alan B. Howes falls into an easy trap and expresses a common view when he describes Volume VII as an "extreme instance of a general tendency." He characterizes the general tendency in the following way: "As Sterne faced the problem of filling up each succeeding installment, he was driven more and more to include a certain amount of really extraneous material, which had much less connection with his really central story than the digressions of volumes one and two had."[1] William Holtz agrees that "the seventh book remains an odd piece in the fabric of [Sterne's] tale and, by a seeming paradox, the only real digression in *Tristram Shandy*."[2] But his argument is more sophisticated than Howes'. He finds in the biographical origins of Volume VII a link between the pictorialist tradition and Sterne's final literary concept. He suggests that the form of *Tristram Shandy* emerged as part of Sterne's desire to deny Time—as it represented death and mortality. From this point of view, Volume VII is seen as allowing Sterne a necessary purgation of the threat of death which, omnipresent, intruded "into the hermetic world of imaginative recall." Once Sterne puts this threat behind him, Holtz explains, he is able to proceed with the familiar narrative form of Volumes VIII and IX.

Howes' error arises from his thwarted expectations of a "central story" that shares the formal and thematic attributes of more traditional fiction. Holtz's mistake grows from his misunderstanding of Sterne's broad philosophical orientation. Actually, Sterne's theme is concerned with the relation of a private reality to a public world that remains largely unknown but wields an incontrovertible power. When we reach the middle of Volume VI, we have been given the negative details of Tristram's life. It is a story of limitation which describes primarily that which he cannot become. The breeching of Tristram is the last biographical incident recorded about the young hero. It stands for the acceptance of his physical and social determination. The mystery of his potency is sealed, and the force of opinion is rec-

1. *Yorick and the Critics: Sterne's Reputation in England, 1760–1868*, p. 35.
2. *Image and Immortality: A Study of Tristram Shandy*, p. 133.

ognized. Since his immediate environment will remain more or less constant and his education—as Walter outlines it in the *Tristrapædia* —is doomed to failure, we are here given a prophetic vision of the man. With the fate of his mind and body largely decided, Tristram turns for understanding and escape to his art: to the last and most important of his romances, the courtship of Uncle Toby and the Widow Wadman. There remains but one major accident that can befall him, one arbitrary and universal condition to be added to the facts of his physical, mental, and emotional life: the recognition of death that brings with it an awareness of time and mortality. It is one of those fundamental paradoxes upon which life turns, giving it meaning while reducing it to absurdity. Tristram must deal with death before he is able to commit himself either to the practice of art or to life itself.

Tristram's tour, a paradigm of his journey through life and a description of his artistic technique, continues along the very thematic and structural paths that have been set in the first six volumes. Tristram's values remain essentially the same, although their area of articulation has changed. Inflexibility and formalism are still primary targets of satire, here exemplified by the jargon and minutiae of travel literature and guide books:

> This town, if we may trust its archives, the authority of which I see no reason to call in question in this place——was *once* no more than a small village belonging to one of the first Counts *de Guines*; and as it boasts at present of no less than fourteen thousand inhabitants, exclusive of four hundred and twenty distinct families in the *basse ville* or suburbs——it must have grown up by little and little, I suppose, to its present size.
>
> Though there are four convents, there is but one parochial church in the whole town; I had not an opportunity of taking its exact dimensions, but it is pretty easy to make a tolerable conjecture of 'em——for as there are fourteen thousand inhabitants in the town, if the church holds them all, it must be considerably large——and if it will not——'tis a very great pity they have not another. . . . (VII.v.484)

It is the human element, unpredictable and immeasurable, which is important, not the geographical fact or the inanimate object, both of which are found worthy of Tristram's best ironic treatment.

There is not a town in all *France*, which in my opinion, looks better in the map, than MONTREUIL;——I own, it does not look so well in the book of post roads; but when you come to see it ——to be sure it looks most pitifully.

There is one thing however in it at present very handsome; and that is the inn-keeper's daughter. . . . (VII.ix.489)

The audacity and vanity which Tristram found to be common to the academician and the professional are common also to the modish traveler in whose voice he now often speaks and with whom the reader is, of course, identified. "——No;——I cannot stop a moment to give you the character of the people——their genius——their manners——their customs——their laws——their religion——their government——their manufactures——their commerce——their finances, with all the resources and hidden springs which sustain them: qualified as I may be, by spending three days and two nights amongst them, and during all that time, making these things the entire subject of my enquiries and reflection——" (VII.xix.502). The deceptive illusions of opinion are again investigated (VII.vii.487), and commonsense is found (as always) to triumph over the theoretical and abstract.

I love the Pythagoreans . . . for their . . . *"getting out of the body in order to think well."* No man thinks right whilst he is in it; blinded as he must be, with his congenial humours . . . REASON is, half of it, SENSE; and the measure of heaven itself is but the measure of our present appetites and concoctions——
——But which of the two, in the present case, do you think to be mostly in the wrong?
You, certainly: quoth she, to disturb a whole family so early. (VII.xiii.493–94)

The problem of communication is also treated in this section, which follows the rest of the novel in indicating the mutual dependence of the epistemological and the aesthetic. The conflict of the mind and the word is comically dramatized in the story of the Abbess of Andoüillets, who is sadly victimized by language as she attempts to move her obstinate mule (VII.xxi–xxv.504–10). In Tristram's sympathetic interchange with an ass, the superiority of intuition to rational, verbal response is underlined (VII.xxxii.523).

In the "poignant" tale of Amanda and Amandus—so sugary on the surface, so acerbic within—we are presented with another ironic comment on the nature of the romantic imagination. It is "a story read of two fond lovers, separated from each other by cruel parents, and by still more cruel destiny" (VII.xxi.520). For twenty years they wander and suffer, searching faithfully for one another. Finally:

> . . . chance unexpected bringing them at the same moment of the night, though by different ways, to the gate of *Lyons* their native city, and each in well-known accents calling out aloud,
> Is *Amandus*   ⎫
>   ⎬   still alive?
> Is my *Amanda* ⎭
> they fly into each others arms, and both drop down dead for joy. (VII.xxxi.521)

The dream is life-sustaining. The imagination builds a world in which it is bearable to live—but always there is Diego's nose, the Widow Wadman's persistent question, Jenny's sexuality, the signing of the Peace of Utrecht: the threats of reality.

It is in Tristram's meeting with the peasant girl Nanette that the polar philosophical possibilities of the novel are brought together and the transitional meaning of the section is focused. The alternatives which Tristram has faced on his tour are essentially the same as those he has found to be the consequence of his early experiences as an ill-fated Shandy, the same as those which he has perceived as social critic and writer: spontaneity or formality, sophistication or innocence, reason or emotion, artifice or nature, commitment or estrangement. Of Nanette he says: "*Viva la joia!* was in her lips——*Viva la joia!* was in her eyes. A transient spark of amity shot across the space betwixt us——she look'd amiable!——Why could I not live and end my days thus? Just disposer of our joys and sorrows, cried I, why could not a man sit down in the lap of content here——and dance, and sing, and say his prayers, and go to heaven with this nut brown maid? Capriciously did she bend her head on one side, and dance up insidious——Then, 'tis time to dance off, quoth I . . . " (VII.xliii. 538). Tristram, unlike the other Shandys, is able to recognize the alternatives with which the world confronts him. His recognition, however, does not at the same time imply freedom. Understanding and action are limited because objectivity and freedom are impossible. His choice is for art, which represents an escape from death through illusion: " . . . at last I danced myself into *Perdrillo*'s pavillion, where pulling a paper of black lines, that I might go on straight forwards, without digression or parenthesis, in my uncle *Toby*'s amours——I begun thus——" (VII.xliii.538). Of course, he cannot go on straight forward "without digression or parenthesis." He cannot achieve a rational art any more than he can control the forms of his life. His decision to conclude his "Life and Opinions" with an account of the amours of uncle Toby and the Widow Wadman adds but another set of ironies to the work's structure.

In the final two volumes, the ironic meaning of Tristram's title is made explicit. Wayne Booth asserts that "it thus seems thoroughly plausible that, from the beginning, Sterne planned the structure of the book as an elaborate and prolonged contradiction of his title page. For this purpose, one major shift of attention, if sufficiently surrounded with a multiplicity of minor shifts, is all that is needed: begin by pretending to tell the life and opinions of Tristram Shandy and end by telling the amours and campaigns of uncle Toby, concluding the whole account four years before the birth of your original hero." He points out, further, that each of the four installments concludes with promises concerning the disclosure of critical events of Tristram's life and the circumstances of uncle Toby's amours.[3] These promises are all fulfilled with the story of Toby's enlightenment and disenchantment.

Tristram does himself admit the important place which the courtship and the revelation of the Widow Wadman's real concern have occupied in his plan: ". . . I have all along been hastening towards this part of it, with so much earnest desire, as well knowing it to be the choicest morsel of what I had to offer to the world . . ." (IX.xxiv. 627). He has given up his opportunity for love and commitment to a life of spontaneous pleasure in order to present this romance—and it proves to be but a new version of old frustrations, misunderstandings, and incapacities. It marks his return to the old concerns and the old symbols in a reassertion of the same values. Given Sterne's orientation, there can be no progression. The Grand Tour was a beginning, but it was only the beginning of a return, a curve in the circle which is finally closed at the end of the ninth volume. In this sense, it would seem that while Tristram seems to frustrate his declared purpose by

3. "Did Sterne Complete *Tristram Shandy?*," p. 180.

telling the story of Uncle Toby's courtship, he is actually providing us with an image of reality that is different in superficial detail but identical in meaning.

The events of the courtship represent another collection of "facts" which are made real through their internalization into the subjective patterns of consciousness. The Widow Wadman is the victim of external circumstances. It is her former lack of good fortune, we are told, which has made her so zealous in the present affair. "It was just as natural for Mrs. *Wadman*, whose first husband was all his time afflicted with a Sciatica, to wish to know how far from the hip to the groin; and how far she was likely to suffer more or less in her feelings, in one case than in the other" (IX.xxvi.636). And that which seems concupiscence in her character is presented as the natural expression of a natural desire in Bridget or the Fair Beguine. It is the social level as well as her lover's predilection which determines the interpretation of her interest.

As for Toby, he is the victim of internal forces of the illusory world he has created. He pays the same lip service to the institution of marriage and parenthood as he does to the institution of war, but he is always ignorant of the reality. It is the simplicity of the ennobling name that attracts him, rather than the complexity of the human articulation. It is in the word "Humanity" that Toby places his trust, a word that is particularly difficult to translate into the coordinates of action; when the abstract is replaced by the concrete presence of physical concerns, the Widow becomes only the most painful of memories for him.

Furthermore, Toby's situation provides an opportunity for the projection of a series of private associations reflecting pragmatic interest (Walter's concern over his economic loss in the event of Toby's marrying and Bridget's interest in forwarding her relationship with Trim) and habitual emotional, imaginative, and rational response. This is but another indication that Sterne attempts, in these last two volumes, to draw his work together, giving a final, purposeful insight into the unity and inevitability of individual action through the repetition of structural and thematic strains.[4]

4. Wayne Booth has been most instrumental in combating popular opinion that *Tristram Shandy* was never really completed but was stopped at an arbitrary point in accordance with the general lack of structure and purposeful thematic movement. He uses materials from Sterne's letters in his proof and draws upon the incidents of the last chapter in Volume IX for most of his internal evidence.

As we have already seen, the story of the Widow and Uncle Toby, the last and longest of the anti-romances, is a comment on the nature of both sexuality and artistic validity. In its telling, Tristram has included echoes of other major digressions. In the colloquy on love and marriage (VIII.xxxiii.585–88) triggered by Uncle Toby's romance and conducted by Walter, Mrs. Shandy, Uncle Toby, Yorick, and Dr. Slop, we are reminded of Trim's reading of the sermon, which afforded another occasion for the demonstration of personality and eccentric belief. Slawkenbergius makes a brief but brilliant return, now explaining in ambiguous terms what it is that a woman looks for when she is about to marry (IX.xxi.624–25). Walter's letter (VIII.xxiv. 590–93), incapable of re-creating its author's attitude in its recipient, is reminiscent of the doomed *Tristrapædia*; and the story of Maria (IX.xxiv.629–31) recalls the manner and matter of the vignettes of Volume VII. The blank page on which the conversation between Uncle Toby and the Widow Wadman is *not* recorded, is a repetition of the graphic tricks which Tristram enjoyed playing earlier in his work (IX.xviii.621). Trim's eloquent flourishing of his stick to indicate the nature of freedom (IX.iv.604) reminds us of Trim's eloquent use of his hat to convey the meaning of mortality. Tristram's digressions—on criticism, on key-holes, on digressions themselves—contain the same kind of material that they contained before. Tristram's discussion of his sickness (VIII.vi.545), of his frustrated romance with Jenny (VIII.xi–xiii.550–51), and of Trim's brother Tom, whose love affair with another widow brings him eventually to the prison of the Inquisition (IX.iv–viii.603–09), similarly recall earlier themes and incidents. And Tristram's "Dedication" to Pitt, which begins Volume IX and specifically looks back to the dedication of the first volume, makes the circular movement of the novel explicit.

It is, however, in the final chapter of the last volume that we find Sterne's purpose most resourcefully revealed. Here, as Wayne Booth points out, the subject matter and allusions of the early chapters are closely paralleled. More than this, the brief section manages to comment on the nature and the implications of the hobbyhorses of the brothers Shandy while giving a brief allegorical account of the critical incidents of Tristram's life. Walter's tirade against the degradation of the sexual act makes eminently clear the intensity of his withdrawal from instinctive and spontaneous behavior into the realm of rationality and sublimation. It also indicates, incidentally, one of the sources of the subjective and metaphorical use of language. It is this that has provided Sterne with one of his principal structural and thematic strains: ". . . and for what reason is it, that all the parts thereof——the congredients——the preparations——the instruments, and whatever serves thereto, are so held as to be conveyed to a cleanly mind by no language, translation, or periphrasis whatever?" (IX. xxxiii.645). The irony of Walter's domestic situation is underlined once more for him, the act of procreation is ". . . a passion, my dear, continued my father, addressing himself to my mother, which couples and equals wise men with fools, and makes us come out of caverns and hiding-places more like satyrs and four-footed beasts than men" (IX.xxxiii.645). It was his sexuality that motivated his marriage, unsuitable in every other way, and it is his marriage that has in turn been responsible for the subversion of his sexuality.

Walter's speech pinpoints too the crucial irony of Toby's hobby: "——The act of killing and destroying a man, continued my father raising his voice——and turning to my uncle *Toby*——you see, is glorious——and the weapons by which we do it are honourable—— We march with them upon our shoulders——We strut with them by our sides,——We gild them——We carve them——We in-lay them ——We enrich them——Nay, if it be but a *scoundril* cannon, we cast an ornament upon the breech of it——" (IX.xxxiii.645). With the final image—the last of the innumerable metaphors connecting war and sexuality—Tristram emphasizes the perversity of a society that honors destruction and denigrates creation. That Toby is the innocent and eccentric representative of such a society is emphasized by the meaning of Obadiah's story; for, with Tristram, Toby is made the victim of society's prudish curiosity and frustration.

The story of Tristram's victimization, with its implications for his uncle and his father, is also brilliantly summarized in this final chapter. Walter's speech looks back to the unfortunate circumstances surrounding Tristram's conception. His thoughts about the feelings of men toward war and the implied connection of these thoughts with Uncle Toby's hobbyhorse, remind us of the events leading up to Tristram's circumcision. All of the ambiguity connected with this accident as well as with Uncle Toby's injury and Walter's inadequacy, is developed in Obadiah's story of the Bull, whose fertility is so sadly in question. The parallel is clearly suggested by Walter's observation to Toby that ". . . this poor Bull of mine, who is as good a Bull as ever p-ss'd, and might have done for *Europa* herself in purer times—— had he but two legs less, might have been driven into Doctors Commons and lost his character——which to a Town Bull, brother *Toby*, is the very same thing as his life————" (IX.xxxiii.646–47). All three, Tristram, Toby, and Walter, might have done for Europa's counterpart "in purer times," and all have been dragged into the court of public opinion, where the reader has sat as one of the judges, and where they have lost, at best, their reputations.

Finally, speaking for herself and for Tristram's reader, Mrs. Shandy asks: "L--d! . . . what is all this story about?——" (IX. xxxiii.647). Yorick's reply has all of the commonsense, the humor, and the meaningful ambiguity that seems appropriate to his role: "A COCK and a BULL, said *Yorick*——and one of the best of its kind, I ever heard" (IX.xxxiii.647). This is indeed a synthesizing statement. As a bit of criticism it brings us, in effect, to the beginning of the work: to the image of Tristram the artist, writing to escape the circumstances of his life, using his art as the alternative to despair once everything else has seemingly been denied him. And, of course, it presents us with his failure. He has produced a "cock and bull" story: a silly and perverse work that structurally describes the chaotic, arbitrary development of his life—and expresses, through the apparent, thematic confusion, a sense of his own lack of understanding.

But still, as Yorick says, it is "one of the best of its kind I ever heard." His opinion is confirmed by the richness of Tristram's last irresistible joke. The word "cock" reminds us of the phallic imagery that has been used throughout the novel to create a sense of linguistic, emotional, and physical frustration. It recalls the central conflict between man's animal and social natures; the phallus comes to stand for man's alienation from himself and from his environment, his tragicomic isolation and aspiration. On one hand, the pun asserts the novel's affinity with the tradition of Rabelais. On the other hand, for the contemporary reader, it seems strangely prophetic—another of the many indications of the extent to which Sterne's vision was philosophically and artistically sophisticated.

Four

Laurence Sterne
and the Contemporary Vision

What, then, is the twentieth-century reader to make of *Tristram Shandy*—this strange rambling work that hides its purpose beneath a cloak of confusion, telling a story not of men's lives but of their minds? And how is the reader to explain the surprising contemporaneousness which stimulates a comparison such as this: "Not till modern times do we find so intelligent an attempt to consider the aesthetic and philosophical implications of the novel. Not till Gide and Proust and James and Joyce and Virginia Woolf is there any comparable picture in fiction of the process of living, of life caught in the very act of Being. Sterne moreover paralleled this with his picture of himself in the process of creating his book. There is in *Tristram Shandy* a three-fold development; the characters as they evolve; the author as he works out his concept; and the reader whom Sterne is educating to understand fiction aright."[1] Sterne's relation to the epistemological and linguistic theories of Locke provides us with the link necessary to our understanding of his relation to the contemporary vision, just as it helped us before to understand his relation to the literary movements of his own time. One discovers that it is in Sterne's commitment to Locke's subjective relativism, in his willingness to extend it into every area of man's intellectual, emotional, and aesthetic life, that Sterne the philosopher looks ahead to some aspects of the thought of Bergson, James, and Freud, the three major philosophical influences on the modern novel. In this way, Sterne the novelist anticipates contemporary literary themes and narrative techniques.

Of the three modern figures it is Bergson who has the closest connection to Locke. It is between them that we find the greatest number of crucial similarities—in their concepts of identity, language, and

1. A. A. Mendilow, *Time and the Novel*, p. 107.

time. There are more fragmentary echoes in James' concept of the "stream of consciousness" and in Freud's definition of the self. Of course, this is not to suggest that the systems of the three men can be equated. It is only an indication of the fact that, in the consideration of the impact of a systematic philosophy upon a literary movement, it is the general orientation in psychological and aesthetic areas which is important. These attributes are translated by the novelist into concrete experiential terms. To the extent that Bergson, James, and Freud shared a general romantic orientation, their influence was shared. To the extent that Bergson articulated this point of view most extensively in aesthetic terms, his influence can be seen as dominant.

Those aspects of Bergson's philosophy that were most relevant to the development of the modern novel were his concept of the self and its external reality, and his attitude toward language. In the *Introduction to Metaphysics*, Bergson tells us that philosophers distinguish two ways in which an object of the external world can be known. The first method is a relative one, for it suggests that we perceive the object from different points of view and describe it in symbolic and conceptual terms. The second technique provides for entrance into the object itself by means of an effort of the imagination or intuitive faculty. It is thus that one is able to attain the absolute, which offers an immediate experience of that which is both unique and ineffable. To analyze the object according to the former method is to reduce it to elements which are known to be common to it and other objects, and is therefore to express the thing as a function of something else. To enter the object by empathizing with it is to possess it completely and unquestioningly.

The ultimate purpose of knowledge and the goal of metaphysics is to grasp the "élan vital"—the creative force driving life to ever higher levels of organization, the unique nature of all animate life and the ultimate principle of existence.[2] This can be accomplished through an act of intuition rather than by the activity of the intellect, through the intuition of the one object which gives us a sense of the creative evolution which is life itself. This object is our own personality. Through introspection we discover a ceaselessly changing process which is the constant, moving, varying, colorful flow of personality. The process is called by Bergson "durée," and is the pure time which is absolute reality revealed in the inner flow of self. Knowledge gained

2. Henri Bergson, *An Introduction to Metaphysics*, pp. 21–22.

by means of self-analysis can in turn be followed by a process of abstraction and conceptualization. It is therefore possible to move from intuition to concept, while the reverse procedure, according to Bergson, is not feasible (pp. 24–29). Metaphysics, therefore, establishes the conclusion that mobility is reality.

Closely bound up with Bergson's "durée" is his concept of memory, which suggests that the memories of past things interpenetrate the present experience. Past and present are joined in a unity of consciousness which is an irreversible flowing to the future. Bertrand Russell, in *A History of Western Philosophy*, points out the extent to which Bergson maintains an idealist position. Russell explains that "his theory of time is seen to be simply a theory which omits time altogether." Bergson is not recognizing a "real" past, but is speaking only of "the present idea of the past." Russell goes on to suggest that this is an instance of a more general confusion "between an act of knowing and that which is known" (pp. 807–8). Since Bergson maintains that all knowledge consists of images, matter and the perception of matter are the same thing.

If we pause here for a moment, it is possible to see some of the ways in which Bergson's view of the self—and its relation to an external reality—was anticipated by Locke. As empiricists, the two shared a basic suspicion of the powers of reason. While Bergson was at times willing to admit the possibility that reason and scientific method could aid the efforts of intuition and metaphysics, he always insisted upon the superiority of intuition in achieving an insight into "truth." Locke viewed the possibilities for knowledge with some scepticism but always maintained his faith in reasonableness—the mind's capability to master abstraction and order experience, given the benefit of education and self-discipline. Locke was unable to embrace the idealist resolution of the mind-matter controversy and his acceptance of a Newtonian universe prevented him from following the implications of his epistemological scepticism. Instead of recognizing the creative functioning of the mind in accordance with its own laws, he persisted in defining learning as discovery or apprehension. His unwillingness to adhere to a total subjectivism involved him in constant contradiction. Of course, to the extent that Bergson attempted to compromise his idealism in his treatment of mind, matter, and expression, he too became involved in contradiction.

In Bergson's insistence upon the turning inward of the individual as the beginning of knowledge, in his view of the constantly changing self which contains its past in its present, in his consequent recognition of the importance of memory, we find some of Locke's fundamental but inadequately developed principles. Locke's theory of association does, after all, give to the memory a specifically originative and synthesizing function. The reflective consciousness determines the irrational, subjective, and unique nature of the self (I.II.xxvii.17;458–59). Identity is the extension of consciousness into the past (I.II.xxvii.16;458). Furthermore, although Locke does seem to define the contents of consciousness as discrete but interrelated units, his formulation of the "train of ideas," with its emphasis upon a personally defined, inner sense of time, corresponds in its general feeling to Bergson's "durée." It is upon this correspondence that Mendilow bases his suggestion that Locke's associationist psychology with its corollary of the time-shift technique had a meaning for Sterne similar to that of Bergson's theory of duration for the modern writer: "They aim at conveying the effect of an all-pervading present of which past and future are part, in preference to an orderly progression in time of separate events" (p. 169).

The empiricist view of reality held by both men determined the nature of their observations about language. W. M. Urban, in his book *Language and Reality*, explains that the high evaluation of language is the underlying assumption of all periods of rationalism and is accompanied by a belief in universals. The low valuation of language, which is discovered in all critical periods of culture, is the underlying assumption of the empiricists and is accompanied by some form of nominalism (pp. 10–12).

Because Locke mediated between the old rationalism and the new empiricism, it is only to be expected that the optimistic scepticism which characterized his appraisal of the powers of reason would characterize his judgments concerning the potentialities of language as well, while Bergson's linguistic philosophy reflected a more acute scepticism. In Bergson's thought, language (both the natural language of everyday speech and the artificial language of the sciences) is the tool of the intellect and the means of conceptualization. It is because of language that we have developed the habit of setting out time in space. It is language which "gives a fixed form to fleeting sensation."[3] It is language which encourages us to see sensation as part of the object itself, to perceive the effect through its cause and through the

---

3. Bergson, *Time and Free Will*, p. 77.

words which translate it. Language makes us believe in the unchange-
ableness of our sensations and often deceives us as to their very
nature.

In this way, language will, for example, denote the deeper, subtly
differentiated states of the self by the same words. And by associating
state with state and object with object, by setting them side by side, it
will fail to translate completely that which our souls experience. Indeed, for Bergson there is no common measure for mind and language.[4] The idea of multiplicity, without its relation to number or
space, though clear for pure reflective thought, cannot be translated
into the language of common sense. Language, in short, is ill suited to
render the subtleties of psychological analysis, the shades of the inner
state, or the multiplicity of the absolute. Although it is useful for the
purpose of science and essential for common communication,[5] the
natural and artificial languages can neither grasp the true reality nor
understand the essence of being. Intuition alone is capable of this.

Bergson is indecisive in establishing the relation of intuition and expression. In *An Introduction to Metaphysics*, he implies that intuition
does not permit of expression: "If there exists any means of possessing a reality absolutely instead of knowing it relatively, of placing
oneself within it instead of looking at it from outside points of view,
of having the intuition instead of making the analysis: in short, of
seizing it without expression, translation, or symbolic representation—metaphysics is that means. Metaphysics, then, is the science
which claims to dispense with symbols" (p. 24). Language is created
by the intellect and is insufficient for the attainment of the realization
of truth. The essence may be grasped—but it cannot be expressed.

Bergson does not, however, consistently take this negative position.
He also suggests that a new language must be sought which will be
derived from the natural language and will consist of a more artistic
means of expression employing metaphor and image in its descriptions. Since one is always conscious of the illusory nature of the
image (never mistaking it for an actual representation) the integrity
of the intuition can be maintained while communication of the absolute is made possible.[6] Clearly, Bergson here is equating metaphysics and poetry. He advocates the use of a poetic form of state-

4. Ibid., pp. 165–66.
5. See Henri Bergson, *Creative Evolution*, pp. 166–68. Here he expressed
a full awareness of some characteristic values of language.
6. *An Introduction to Metaphysics*, pp. 27–28.

ment, comparing the metaphysician's goal with the poet's desire to catch a fleeting glimpse of a mobile reality. The implications for art are obviously positive, since Bergson gives to the poetic insight a new validity and technique, as surely as he has given to it, with his emphasis upon the self, a new subject.

If we now consider Sterne's attitude toward language as it develops from his reading of Locke and anticipates Bergson, we again find strong similarities to Bergson's more extreme philosophy. Sterne's scepticism extends to all knowledge. He reveals the fallacy underlying all usage, all interpretation, all definition. Speech, like perception, is incapable of offering any but the individual, relative truth. All language is as susceptible to interpretation as the emptiest sound, the most ambiguous exclamation—as susceptible to interpretation as Phutatorius' cry of "zounds" in response to the surprising presence of a hot chestnut inside his breeches. The nominalism which is only suggested by Locke is extended by Sterne until language is revealed to be at the root of the chaos, the confusion, and the misunderstandings of everyday life and intellectual discourse.

Furthermore, the tragedy of the Shandys—which is derived from Sterne's image of Locke—is not unlike the plight of Bergson's misdirected intellectual. It lies, for example, in Walter's absolute truths formulated by reason, in his faith in concepts which are imposed upon the faulty, misleading, and subjective data of experience. It lies in the belief of each of the Shandy males in his own subjective vision as an objectively valid version of reality. Although Sterne does not suggest the possibilities of intuition in forwarding the cause of formal knowledge or metaphysical understanding, he does, however, with his theory of empathy, make possible meaningful and ethical human relationships that transcend the limitations of language. Further, the uneasy dualism of Bergson's view has its counterpart in Sterne's alternative to mute sympathy—his celebration in Tristram of wit, which, by employing the imagination to perceive and using metaphor and symbol to express, is alone capable of capturing and retaining the rich, elusive meaning of multiplicity and ambiguity.

In those areas in which Locke's and Sterne's thought seems to be prophetic of Bergson's philosophy, it seems also to be prophetic of some limited aspects of the writings of William James and Freud. This can, of course, be traced to the fact that James and Freud developed independently, along specifically psychological lines, those relevant elements of Bergson's metaphysics.

Although the theories of Bergson and James seem to converge in the sphere of literary influence, James' theory of consciousness preceded Bergson's, which, nevertheless, was apparently developed independently.[7] In the ninth chapter of his *Principles of Psychology*, James denies the subject-object dualism which is a source of contradiction in the epistemologies of both Locke and Bergson. His "radical empiricism" insists that everything is composed of "pure experience" which cannot be atomistically described. Here James introduces his famous metaphor for the functioning of consciousness—a metaphor that has been used to describe the narrative method of such writers as Proust, Gide, Joyce, and Virginia Woolf: "Consciousness, then, does not appear to itself chopped up in bits. Such words as 'chain' or 'train' do not describe it fitly as it presents itself in the first instance. It is jointed; it flows. A 'river' or a 'stream' is the metaphor by which it is most naturally described. *In talking of it hereafter, let us call it the stream of thought, of consciousness, or of subjective life*" (p. 154). James emphasizes the importance of the experience of the interior rhythm which exists apart from language and, as sensibility, plays an important role in creative functions. "The difference in the rate of change lies at the basis of a difference of subjective states of which we ought immediately to speak. When the rate is slow we are aware of the object of our thought in a comparatively restful and stable way. When rapid, we are aware of a passage, a relation, a transition *from* it, or *between* it and something else. As we take, in fact, a general view of the wonderful stream of our consciousness, what strikes us first is this different pace of its parts" (pp. 157–58). His conception is of the fluidity of consciousness, of the sensible perception of the flux, and of the equation of memory and identity: "Experience is remoulding us every moment, and our mental reaction on every given thing is really a resultant of our experience of the whole world up to that date" (p. 152). All are important in providing the novel of subjectivity that dedicates itself to the painstaking study and re-creation of consciousness, with its motivating impulse and theoretical framework.

7. In 1884 (*Mind*, 9:1–26, 188–205), James published two articles which put forth two distinctive doctrines. The first, which was later elaborated upon in the ninth chapter of his *Principles of Psychology*, offered a conception of thought as a stream in which relations are the immediate data of perception, and the second described emotion as organic sensation. Bergson, in his first book, *Time and Free Will* (1889), cites the second article. Later, in an essay in *Revue Philosophique*, 55:229, he denied any knowledge of the first.

It is, of course, impossible to separate the later influence of James from that of Bergson. Both make themselves felt in the same areas and both elaborate further the growing romanticism that ruled all spheres of intellectual investigation. Still another related elaboration of this same tradition can be found in the work of Freud and the psychoanalytic movement, as Lionel Trilling suggests, when he traces the tradition back to 1762 and Diderot's *Rameau's Nephew*: " . . . psychoanalysis is one of the culminations of the Romanticist literature of the nineteenth century. . . . this literature, despite its avowals, was itself scientific in at least the sense of being passionately devoted to a research into the self."[8] In fact, the Freudian view of character and the unconscious is not, in some respects, different from that suggested by Locke. There are, throughout *An Essay Concerning Human Understanding*, frequent if vague allusions to irrational elements of the mind that exert an influence which, while not totally explicable, are in some way connected with an individual's experience. In fact, as Ernest Tuveson points out, Locke goes beyond this and suggests, in his edition of 1690 (I.ii.i.22;140–41), that children acquire simple ideas early, perhaps in the womb, which persist even though the mind cannot be aware of them. There is, in these unremembered ideas which influence a mind that is ignorant of their presence, some implication of the unconscious.[9] There is the same implication in Locke's discussion of the irrational nature of association, which can, in its most extreme forms, become a kind of madness.

Further, Locke's concept of identity as a function of memory is prophetic of Freud's view, just as it is an earlier, simplified form of the definitions of self offered by James and Bergson. All of these men give us a theory of consciousness in which the past is contained in the present, affecting behavior and determining emotional and intellectual response. It is in this way that the psychoanalytic emphasis upon the reconstruction of the self is made aesthetically meaningful. It is only through the analysis of the totality of the individual's life that we are able to achieve a valid understanding of his personality. This method of analysis demands in art, as well as in psychology, the creation of a new form. It is therefore fascinating, although not really surprising, that the form which Sterne developed

8. "Freud and Literature," p. 677.
9. "Locke and the Dissolution of the Ego," p. 170.

as a result of his interpretation of Locke, should be in many ways similar to those adopted by the novelists who were influenced by Bergson, James, and Freud. The brief readings below will suggest some of the similarities.

Germaine Brée gives us the key to the nature of the development when she writes that Gide, in search of the novel, "found that the only novel worth writing is always one and the same—the novel that reveals the inadequacy of all fiction when it is confronted with life. Gide is not a creator but a destroyer of fictional worlds."[10] For Sterne and the stream-of-consciousness writers of this century, the public symbols and social values of the conventional novel proved inadequate to the task of conveying the complexity of psychological truth. In order to describe a world which could have no existence apart from the agents who internalized it, the artist established a new relationship with his work—a relationship that involved him as a man and as a writer as well as a philosopher concerned with basic metaphysical, epistemological, and aesthetic problems. It is in his own image that Sterne creates Tristram, as Joyce creates Stephen; Proust, Marcel; and Gide, Edouard. It is in relation to the surrogate artist that all of the characters are defined. Although they develop identities of their own, it is to the central figure that they are always referred, to their place in the continual flux and reflexivity of his consciousness. It is with profit that we compare Sterne's use of Tristram with Gide's use of Edouard in *The Counterfeiters*, here described by Brée: "The problem Gide raises is the problem of maintaining an inner integrity by 'composing' honestly out of a double reality one's individual self and the independent workings of the world around one, a self-evaluation that is never final and that is essentially a search for a true form of living" (p. 38). And the similarities are as great and as interesting between Sterne and Proust, for Marcel looks, with Tristram, into himself in order to find a principle of unity that will give order to the constantly changing self and meaning to the external world that cannot be objectively known. Despite the sophistication of Proust's concept of memory and the mastery with which he communicates and brings together the elements of Marcel's search for identity, the underlying assumptions of his work ally him with Locke.

10. Germaine Brée and Margaret Guiton, *An Age of Fiction: The French Novel from Gide to Camus*, p. 39.

In the stream-of-consciousness novel the rhythms of the mind replace the movement of a conventional plot sequence. Mendilow describes the action of this psychological novel as ". . . the replacing of causality on the plane of action by pure sequence on the plane of thought-feeling—a kind of picaresque novel of the day-dreaming mind" (p. 160). Sterne, with his associationist-impressionism, prefigured the time-shift technique that came in the wake of Bergson and James. The confused chronology, the complicated system of cross-references, the unconventional syntax, and the eccentric development of language are all part of the method that Virginia Woolf, for one, consciously adopted. Further, Sterne's treatment of time was, as we have seen, a natural extension of his concepts of the nature of the self and the role of the artist, and it was no less prophetic than these.

Indeed, Hans Castorp in *The Magic Mountain* could well be speaking for Tristram-Sterne as well as for Bergson or James when he says:

> But after all, time isn't actual! When it seems long to you, then it *is* long; when it seems short, why, then it is short. But how long, or how short, it actually is, that nobody knows.
>
> . . .
>
> We say of time that it passes. Very good, let it pass. But to be able to measure it—wait a minute: to be susceptible of being measured, time must flow evenly, but who ever said it did that? As far as our consciousness is concerned it doesn't, we only assume that it does for the sake of convenience; and our units of measurement are purely arbitrary, sheer conventions.[11]

Similarly, Proust's attempts to overcome Time, to reach self-definition through the analysis of memory, and to grasp the images of memory through a process of association are not, on the surface, unlike Sterne's attempts—although the articulations of Proust's concept are clearly more complex. Virginia Woolf's emphasis on psychological time, marked by the mind's reception of and response to impressions, is but an extension of Sterne's associational technique and testifies to the truth of her claims of indebtedness. All of the writer-surrogates share with Tristram the painful dilemma he finds

11. Thomas Mann, *The Magic Mountain*, p. 66.

himself in at Auxerre. Here all the dimensions of time, which he attempts to maintain distinctly, threaten to converge, burying him in confusion and defeating his attempts at self-definition: ". . . I am this moment walking across the market place of *Auxerre* with my father and my uncle *Toby*, in our way back to dinner——and I am this moment also entering *Lyons* with my post-chaise broke into a thousand pieces——and I am moreover this moment in a handsome pavillion built by *Pringello*, upon the banks of the *Garonne*, which Mons. *Sligniac* has lent me, and where I now sit rhapsodizing all these affairs" (VI.xxviii.516).

It follows as well, that Locke's and Bergson's suspicion of language, their sense of the difficulties of expressing that which is intuitive or unique in experience, should be reflected in the writing of both Sterne and his modern counterparts. Because the simultaneity and ambiguity of experience had now to be communicated, the emphasis came to be placed on the connotative and impressionistic aspects of language. It is in *Ulysses* and *Finnegans Wake* that we find the most extreme and exciting development of Sterne's linguistic experimentation.[12] Again a greater sophistication gives rise to a complexity of technique that is quantitatively different from Sterne's, but grows from common roots and has a common goal. While Joyce's distortions of language develop from a careful differentiation and description of the conscious, subconscious, and unconscious levels of mind, and while they are woven together to form an incredibly patterned tapestry of meaning, the effects that they achieve are in many ways similar to those that result from Sterne's more random and limited method.

The germs of parallel development are found also in the concept of character which Sterne shares, in a general way, with the modern psychological novelist. Martin Turnell describes the nature of Proust's "prisoner-hero": ". . . he is the passive victim who is exposed to almost every conceivable kind of pressure and obsession known to human society. For he is the prisoner . . . of emotions, habits, of his own sensibility and, ultimately, of time."[13] The applicability of this definition to Sterne's characters, as well as to those of Proust, Joyce, Gide, and Virginia Woolf, is clear. Similarly, Turnell's definition of Marcel as "the artist-prisoner whose only salvation is in his voca-

12. It is interesting to note that Joyce makes specific mention of Tristram in the second paragraph of *Finnegans Wake*.
13. *The Novel in France*, p. 375.

tion" is applicable to Tristram as it is to all of the artist-hero figures who dominate and unify the stream-of-consciousness novel.

Because isolation is the result of man's attempt to communicate with other men and because futility and frustration result from his attempts to order and control his external reality, the themes of the modern psychological novel, like those of *Tristram Shandy*, are given a subjective reference. The concern is always with attitude rather than event. Language, death, and sexuality are functions of the self, modes of apprehension, expressions of personality. The characters do not act. They are acted upon and must only learn how best to deal with their illusions of freedom. The dilemma is not one which permits resolution. For Virginia Woolf, self-discovery is generally accepted as a prelude to death. For Joyce, as for Sterne, there can be no self-discovery. There is only the endless repetition of the quest.

Sterne, having interpreted Locke freely and prophetically, simultaneously created the stream-of-consciousness novel and brought it to the farthest thematic and structural limits possible for the eighteenth century. It remained for Joyce to explore definitively the formal possibilities of the genre. In *Ulysses* and, more particularly, in *Finnegans Wake*, he produced novels that paralleled *Tristram Shandy* in their eccentricity and originality. But although Sterne's promise seems ultimately fulfilled with Joyce's novels, the influences and the vision were echoed still again and with a new freshness in the "Theatre of the Absurd."

The dramatists whose works can be included in this group (Beckett, Ionesco, Genet, Adamov, and Tardieu are most representative), write antidramas in much the same way as Sterne and Joyce can be said to have written antinovels. Setting out to portray man in his absurdity, bereft of freedom, meaningful language, and valid relationships, they must convey a sense of the futility of gesture, speech, and action, a sense of total frustration in the face of complete irrationality. It is Sterne compounded and Joyce purified. We are given a nightmare world in which there is no time, no place, no communication, no identity. All of Sterne's paradoxes are exaggerated, the ironies heightened.

Indeed, the parallels between *Tristram Shandy* and this theatrical movement are many. The dominant tragedy with which the dramatists of the absurd, as well as Sterne and Joyce, concern themselves, is that which grows out of the failure of communication. Tristram says of Toby: " 'twas not by ideas,——by heaven! his life was put in jeopardy by words" (II.1.87). Thus Ionesco calls *The Bald Soprano* "a tragedy of language," describing it as "a kind of play or anti-play, that is, a parody of a play, a comedy of comedy." Similarly, Martin Esslin describes another of Ionesco's plays, *The Lesson*, as ". . . a demonstration of the basic impossibility of communication—words cannot convey meanings because they leave out of account the personal associations they carry for each individual."[14]

Samuel Beckett also takes the disintegration of language as one of his major themes, while using it in his plays as a dominant stylistic device. With Sterne, Beckett uses cliché, double-entendre, metaphor, and pun to indicate the inherent ambiguity of language, as well as the subconscious conflicts of the human mind. With them, he uses the rambling, disconnected monologue as a sign of a general condition of isolation in which man is trapped while always attempting to establish external connections. With them he wrenches grammatical and syntactical structure, both as a result of and a metaphor for the absence of rational order in social, psychological, and even metaphysical relationships.

The similarities that exist, then, between Sterne and both the dramatists of the absurd and contemporary stream-of-consciousness novelists, are similarities of a philosophical, psychological, and artistic nature, interesting because of their separation in time and independence of development. Indeed, it is just because the interest is so great that we can be betrayed into forgetting the fundamental ways in which *Tristram Shandy* is a work of the eighteenth rather than the twentieth century. Just as Locke mediated between the old rationalism and the new empiricism, denying the existence of innate ideas while maintaining his faith in reasonableness, so too did Sterne look back to the orientation and methods of the satirists, while accomplishing the creation of a new kind of novel. Just as Sterne was able to comprehend and follow the implications of Locke's ideas while still maintaining himself as artist rather than philosopher, so too does his work resemble closely the work of those who followed in the tradition of Bergson, while always maintaining an identity that is unique. Ionesco's statement about the artist's relationship to philosophy is relevant here: ". . . since the artist apprehends reality directly, he is a true philosopher. And it is the broadness, the depth, the sharpness of his philosophical vision, his living philosophy, which

14. *The Theatre of the Absurd*, p. 95.

determines his greatness. The fine quality of works of art comes from the fact that this philosophy is 'living,' that it is life and not abstract thought. One philosophy perishes when a new philosophy, a new system, surpasses it. The living philosophy of works of art, on the contrary, do not invalidate one another. That is why they can co-exist. The great masterpieces, the great poets, seem to justify one another, complete one another, confirm one another."[15]

The differences seem largely to be a matter of degree. For example, while Sterne suggests some of the psychological roots and motivations of his characters, his technique is to reveal them rather than to allow them to develop. Tristram's process of introspection is concerned, in large measure, with things external to his psyche, events in which he has not even been involved. In its form *Tristram Shandy* does not achieve the consistencies which characterize those works which we have considered so quickly. It lacks the extraordinarily integrated fertility of *Ulysses*, the perfect complexity of Proust, the taut purity of the Theatre of the Absurd. Although Sterne is concerned with the exaggerated effect, the grotesquery of human nature, the humor of burlesque, the lunacy of the absurd, he would not envision the extreme that Ionesco advocates: "Push everything to a state of paroxysm, there where the sources of tragedy lie. Create a theatre of violence, violently comic, violently dramatic" (pp. 17–18). And while Sterne ironically entitled his work *The Life and Opinions of Tristram Shandy*, he is not so ironic as Ionesco, who calls his play *The Bald Soprano* because "no soprano, bald or otherwise, appears in it."[16]

That which makes Sterne so astonishingly contemporary is the sense of relativity, the wise acceptance of absurdity, that is a natural outgrowth of radical empiricism. His sense of absurdity extended to include the futility of human reason, the uselessness of language, the hopelessness of aspiration. Tristram seeks with the antihero of the contemporary world an answer to the unanswerable question, "Who am I?": an escape from the inescapable fact that is himself. "Inconsistent soul that man is!——languishing under wounds, which he has the power to heal!——his whole life a contradiction to his knowledge!" (III.xxi.203). This is the paradox of Walter's life, of Toby's life, of Yorick's life. For Sterne it was the paradox of Locke

15. "Discovering the Theatre," pp. 17–18.
16. "The Tragedy of Language," p. 11.

as well. Thus, his irony was not limited to petty concerns and small men. Its implications were cosmic. Ultimately it is Sterne's awareness of the aspiration and the eternal frustration that gives his novel its sense of tragedy. It is his insistence upon the commonplace, incongruous roots of the aspiration that makes his work comic. With this peculiarly modern, tragi-comic quality, *Tristram Shandy* demands its place as a profoundly serious comment on the human condition. As Sigurd Burckhardt points out, "Sterne had learned from Swift. As the last irony of *A Modest Proposal* is that it is *not* ironic, that—society being what it is—Swift's ghastly humanitarianism is genuine and an ironic reading merely an evasion of his cruelly literal point, so Sterne's final joke is again and again that he is not joking."[17]

It is in his role of satirist that Sterne identifies himself as a writer of the eighteenth century. In his relation to the reader, in his critical analysis of modes of thought, in his insistence upon participation, he is allied with the Augustans: deeply critical, sharply ironic, and, in his view of wit and imagination, ultimately optimistic. Sterne does, in the fascinating complexity of *Tristram Shandy*, demand a large price of his reader, and he does at times verge on complete disaster. But just as Tristram triumphs because he must persist, creating through the fertility of his imagination a sense of the impenetrable multiplicity, so does *Tristram Shandy* itself emerge as a monument to the creative power of art. In this sense the novel does become at last a dialogue between Sterne and the reader, a dialogue from which the reader after much difficulty has profited greatly. Therefore, we can ask of *Tristram Shandy*, as Northrop Frye asks of *Finnegans Wake*: "Who then is the hero who achieves the permanent quest. . . . No character in the book itself seems a likely candidate; yet one feels that this book gives us something more than the merely irresponsible irony of a turning cycle. Eventually it dawns on us that it is the reader who achieves the quest; the reader who, to the extent that he masters the book of Doublends Jined, is able to look down on its rotation, and see its form as something more than rotation."[18]

There is, of course, always the danger that the contemporary reader will find more in this ambiguous and paradoxical work than its author could himself have conceived. The greater danger is that

17. "Tristram Shandy's Law of Gravity," pp. 70–71.
18. *Anatomy of Criticism*, p. 324.

we should, in our pride of complexity, forget the joy and the love of Sterne's work; for Sterne was, above all, an apostle of these. The final irony which we should consider, therefore, is this: he who wrote a work that seems to us so prophetic in its awareness of multiplicity, so incisive in its ironic vision, so brilliant in its complexity of execution, was a confirmed believer in the simplest of truths.

Selected Bibliography

Aaron, R. I. *The Theory of Universals.* Oxford, 1952.

Alter, Robert. *Rogue's Progress.* Cambridge, 1969.

————. "*Tristram Shandy* and the Game of Love." *American Scholar* 37 (1968):316–23.

Auerbach, Eric. *Mimesis*, trans. Willard Trask. New York, 1957.

Baird, Theodore. "The Time Scheme of *Tristram Shandy* and a Source." *PMLA* 51 (1936):303–20.

Battestin, Martin. *The Moral Basis of Fielding's Art.* Wesleyan, Connecticut, 1959.

Bergson, Henri. *Creative Evolution*, trans. Arthur Mitchell. New York, 1944.

————. *An Introduction to Metaphysics*, trans. T. E. Hulme. New York, 1953.

————. *Time and Free Will*, trans. F. L. Pogson. London, 1917.

Berkeley, George. "Concerning Human Knowledge." *The English Philosophers from Bacon to Mill.* Ed. Edwin A. Burtt. New York, 1939.

Booth, Wayne C. "Did Sterne Complete *Tristram Shandy?*" *Modern Philology* 48 (1951):172–83.

————. "Distance and Point of View; An Essay in Classification." *Essays in Criticism* 11 (1961):60–79.

————. *The Rhetoric of Fiction.* Chicago, 1961.

————. "The Self-Conscious Narrator in Comic Fiction before *Tristram Shandy.*" *PMLA* 67 (1952):162–85.

Brée, Germaine, and Guiton, Margaret. *An Age of Fiction: The French Novel from Gide to Camus.* New Brunswick, New Jersey, 1957.

Brown, R. C. "Laurence Sterne and Virginia Woolf: A Study in Literary Continuity." *University of Kansas City Review* 25 (1959):153–59.

Burckhardt, Sigurd. "*Tristram Shandy's* Law of Gravity." *ELH* 28 (1961): 70–88.

Cash, Arthur H. "The Lockean Psychology of *Tristram Shandy.*" *ELH* 22 (1955):125–35.

Croll, Morris W. "The Baroque Style in Prose." *Studies in English Philology.* Ed. Kemp Malone and Martin B. Rund. Minneapolis, 1929.

Cross, Wilbur L. *The Life and Times of Laurence Sterne.* New Haven, 1929.

Daiches, David. *The Novel and the Modern World.* Chicago, 1960.

Dilworth, Ernest Nevin. *The Unsentimental Journey of Laurence Sterne.* New York, 1948.

Esslin, Martin. *The Theatre of the Absurd.* New York: Anchor Books, 1961.

————. "The Theatre of the Absurd." *The Tulane Drama Review* 4 (1960): 3–15.

Farrell, William S. "Nature vs. Art as a Comic Pattern in *Tristram Shandy.*" *ELH* 30 (1963):16–35.

Fluchère, Henri. *Laurence Sterne, de l'homme à l'oeuvre.* Paris, 1961.

——. *Laurence Sterne: From Tristram to Yorick,* trans. and abridged by Barbara Bray. Oxford, 1965.

Frame, Donald. *Montaigne's Discovery of Man.* New York, 1955.

Fredman, Alice. *Diderot and Sterne.* New York, 1955.

Frye, Northrop. *Anatomy of Criticism.* Princeton, 1957.

Goldberg, M. A. "Moll Flanders: Christian Allegory in a Hobbesian Mode." *University Review* 33 (1967):267–78.

Hammond, Lansing Van Der Heyden. *Laurence Sterne's "Sermons of Mr. Yorick."* New Haven, 1948.

Harding, M. E. *Journey into Self.* New York, 1956.

Harper, Kenneth E. "A Russian Critic and *Tristram Shandy.*" *Modern Philology* (November 1954):52–59.

Hartley, Lodwick. *Laurence Sterne in the Twentieth Century: An Essay and Bibliography of Sternean Studies 1900–1965.* Chapel Hill, 1966.

——. *This Is Lorence.* Chapel Hill, 1943.

Holland, Norman N. "The Laughter of Laurence Sterne." *Hudson Review* 9 (1956):422–30.

Holtz, William V. *Image and Immortality: A Study of Tristram Shandy.* Providence, 1971.

Howes, Alan B. *Yorick and the Critics: Sterne's Reputation in England, 1760–1868.* New Haven, 1958.

Hume, David. *A Treatise of Human Nature.* Ed. L. A. Selby-Bigge. Oxford, 1888.

Ionesco, Eugene. "Discovering the Theatre." *The Tulane Drama Review* 4 (1959):3–18.

——. "The Tragedy of Language." *The Tulane Drama Review* 4 (1960): 10–13.

James, William. *The Principles of Psychology.* Great Books of the Western World, vol. 53. Ed. Robert Hutchins. Chicago, 1955.

Jefferson, D. W. "*Tristram Shandy* and its Tradition." *The Pelican Guide to English Literature,* vol. 4. Ed. Boris Ford. Baltimore, 1957.

——. "*Tristram Shandy* and the Tradition of Learned Wit." *Essays in Criticism* 1 (1951):225–48.

Kallen, Horace M. *William James and Henri Bergson.* Chicago, 1914.

Karl, Frederick R. "Waiting for Beckett: Quest and Re-Quest." *The Sewanee Review* 62 (1961):661–76.

Kernan, Alvin. *The Cankered Muse.* New Haven, 1959.

Kettle, Arnold. *An Introduction to the English Novel.* New York, 1960.

Knox, Norman. *The Word Irony and Its Context, 1600–1755.* Durham, 1961.

Lehman, B. H. "Of Time, Personality, and the Author: A Study of *Tristram Shandy.*" *University of California Studies in the Comic* (1941):233–50.

Locke, John. *An Essay Concerning Human Understanding,* vols. 1–2. Ed. A. C. Fraser. Oxford, 1894.

Maclean, Kenneth. *John Locke and English Literature of the Eighteenth Century.* New Haven, 1936.

Mann, Thomas. *The Magic Mountain.* New York, 1924.

Mendilow, A. A. *Time and the Novel.* New York, 1952.

Meyerhoff, Hans. *Time in Literature.* Berkeley, 1955.

Morris, O. R. *Locke, Berkeley, Hume.* Oxford, 1931.

New, Melvyn. *Laurence Sterne as Satirist.* Gainesville, Florida, 1969.

Parish, Charles. "The Nature of Mr. Tristram Shandy, Author." *Boston University Studies in English* 5 (1961):74–90.

Paulson, Ronald. *Theme and Structure in Swift's* "Tale of a Tub." New Haven, 1960.

Piper, William. *Lawrence Sterne*. New York, 1965.

Price, Martin. *Swift's Rhetorical Art*. New Haven, 1953.

Putney, Rufus. "The Evolution of *A Sentimental Journey*." *Philological Quarterly* 19 (1940):349–69.

Read, Herbert. *The Sense of Glory*. Cambridge, 1929.

Reid, Ben. "The Sad Hilarity of Sterne." *Virginia Quarterly Review* 32 (1956): 107–30.

Russell, Bertrand. *A History of Western Philosophy*. New York, 1964.

Russell, H. K. "Tristram Shandy and the Technique of the Novel." *Studies in Philology* 42 (1955):581–95.

Sallé, Jean-Paul. "A Source of Sterne's Concept of Time." *The Review of English Studies* 6 (1955):180–82.

Singleton, M. K. "Trismegistic Tenor and Vehicle in Sterne's *Tristram Shandy*." *Papers on Language and Literature* 4 (1968).

Skornia, H. J. "Charles Sorel as a Precursor of Realism." *PMLA* 56 (1941): 379–94.

Stedmond, J. M. *The Comic Art of Laurence Sterne*. Toronto, 1967.

———. "Genre and Tristram Shandy." *Philological Quarterly* 38 (1959): 37–51.

———. "Style and *Tristram Shandy*." *Modern Language Quarterly* 20 (1959): 243–51.

Sterne, Laurence. *Letters*. Ed. Lewis P. Curtis. Oxford, 1935.

———. *The Life and Opinions of Tristram Shandy, Gentleman*. Ed. James A. Work. New York, 1940.

———. *A Sentimental Journey Through France and Italy*. Ed. Gardner D. Stout, Jr. Berkeley, 1967.

———. *The Sermons of Mr. Yorick*. Oxford, 1927.

Stevick, Phillip. *The Chapter in Fiction: Theories of Narrative Division*. Syracuse, 1970.

Stout, Gardner D., Jr. "Yorick's *Sentimental Journey*: A Comic Pilgrim's Progress for the Man of Feeling." *ELH* 30 (1963).

Swift, Jonathan. *The Prose Works of Jonathan Swift*. Ed. Herbert Davis. Oxford, 1939.

Thayer, J. "Laurence Sterne in Germany." *Columbia University Germanic Studies* 2 (1905):192–206.

Towers, A. R. "Sterne's Cock and Bull Story." *ELH* 23 (March 1957):12–29.

Traugott, John. *Tristram Shandy's World: Sterne's Philosophical Rhetoric*. Berkeley, 1954.

Trilling, Lionel. "Freud and Literature." *Literary Opinion in America*. Ed. Morton D. Zabel. New York, 1951.

Turnell, Martin. *The Novel in France*. New York, 1951.

Tuveson, Ernest L. *The Imagination as a Means of Grace*. Berkeley, 1960.

———. "Locke and the Dissolution of the Ego." *Modern Philology* 52 (1955):159–74.

Urban, William Marshall. *Language and Reality*. New York, 1939.

Watkins, W. B. C. *Perilous Balance*. Princeton, 1939.

Watt, Ian. "The Ironic Tradition in Augustan Prose from Swift to Johnson."

Restoration and Augustan Prose, papers delivered by James Sutherland and Ian Watt at the Third Clark Library Seminar, July 14, 1956. Los Angeles, 1956.

―――. "Realism in the Novel." *Essays in Criticism* 2 (October 1952):376–96.

―――. *The Rise of the Novel*. Berkeley, 1957.

Williamson, George. "The Rhetorical Pattern of Neo-Classical Wit." *Modern Philology* 33 (1935):55–81.

―――. *The Senecan Amble*. Chicago, 1951.

Worcester, David. *The Art of Satire*. Cambridge, Mass., 1940.

Work, James A. "The Indebtedness of Tristram Shandy to Certain English Authors: 1670–1740." Ph.D. dissertation, Yale University, 1934.

Index